371.9
GRE
18976

Bringing Up a Challenging Child at Home

D0865935

D 22 MAR 2023

of related interest

Asperger's Syndrome
A Guide for Parents and Professionals
Tony Attwood
ISBN 1 85302 557 1

Pretending to be Normal
Living with Asperger's Syndrome
Liane Holliday Willey
Foreword by Tony Attwood
ISBN 1 85302 749 9

When I'm Away From Home
Jean Camis
ISBN 1 85302 898 3

Behavioural Concerns and Autistic Spectrum Disorders
Explorations and Strategies for Change
John Clements and Ewa Zarkowska
ISBN 1 85302 742 1

Marching to a Different Tune
Diary about an ADHD Boy
Jacky Fletcher
ISBN 1 85302 810 X

**Understanding and Supporting Children with Emotional
and Behavioural Difficulties**
Edited by Paul Cooper
ISBN 1 85302 666 2 pb
ISBN 1 85302 665 4 hb

Eating an Artichoke
A Mother's Perspective on Asperger's Syndrome
Echo Fling
ISBN 1 85302 711 1

Bringing Up a Challenging Child at Home
When Love is not Enough

Jane Gregory

Jessica Kingsley Publishers
London and Philadelphia

All rights reserved. No paragraph of this publication may be reproduced, copied or transmitted save with written permission of the Copyright Act 1956 (as amended), or under the terms of any licence permitting limited copying issued by the Copyright Licensing Agency, 33–34 Alfred Place, London WC1E 7DP. Any person who does any unauthorised act in relation to this publication may be liable to prosecution and civil claims for damages.

The right of Jane Gregory to be identified as author of this work has been asserted by her in accordance with the Copyright, Designs and Patents Act 1988.

First published in the United Kingdom in 2000 by
Jessica Kingsley Publishers Ltd
116 Pentonville Road,
London N1 9JB, England
and
325 Chestnut Street,
Philadelphia, PA 19106, USA

www.jkp.com

371.9
GRE
18976

Copyright © 2000 Jane Gregory

Library of Congress Cataloging in Publication Data
A CIP catalog record for this book is available from the Library of Congress

British Library Cataloguing in Publication Data
A CIP catalogue record for this book is available from the British Library

AYLESBURY COLLEGE

LEARNING RESOURCES

CENTRE

ISBN 1 85302 874 6

Printed and Bound in Great Britain by
Athenaeum Press, Gateshead, Tyne and Wear

Contents

Part 3. Therapy, Practical Help and Support

Preface

Chrissy is petite and graceful with a great sense of fun. She looks more like an eleven-year-old – a female Peter Pan – than a teenager. She has a sweetness about her that draws people to her. Like many children with disabilities, Chrissy touches people's hearts with her exuberance, affectionate nature and beaming smile. Her different way of looking at life makes people laugh; everyone who knows her can recall something funny she has said or done. People rarely forget Chrissy once they meet her – not always for the right reasons!

Her attractiveness makes her challenging behaviour, especially the self-harm, all the more disturbing to witness. She has outbursts that last for up to three hours at a time. They are a recurring theme in her life, as much a part of her as her epilepsy. To see her wild-eyed, wringing her hands as she struggles for control, is heart wrenching.

I believed Chrissy's challenging behaviour was unique or, at least, very rare. She has done everything from eating her own faeces to kicking in my car windscreen. Now I know that there are other families like ours living with a learning disabled child they love dearly, but coping with the nightmare of their child's challenging behaviour.

Parents of non-disabled children may wonder how we cope, and claim: 'I could not do it.' We remind them that we thought we had babies just like theirs until the special needs and challenging behaviour became apparent. Like them, we formed bonds with our child and had hopes and dreams for the future. Our perspectives are different; their children's casual accomplishments are our child's lifetime victories. But, despite the sadness and grief we experienced on learning of our child's disability, our love for our child remains undiminished even when confronted with behaviour we find abhorrent.

It has taken us 15 years to gain any semblance of normality to family life, and to understand why Chrissy's challenging behaviour occurs and how best to deal with it. Many professionals use the terms 'challenging behaviour' and 'delayed development' without fully explaining what they mean. GPs, social workers and health visitors are the parents' first points of contact. Few professionals know about the complexities of challenging behaviour and learning difficulties because they may only come across one such person in their career. This often leads to communication difficulties between families and professionals, leaving parents feeling they are not being listened to.

Parents struggling to cope at home with challenging children complain that outside help only becomes available in an emergency. By then the challenging behaviour is ingrained and more difficult to modify. Divorce is all too common in families where there is a learning disabled child, and it is often the mother who is left coping alone. If family breakdown occurs, social factors such as divorce and poverty contribute to the problem behaviour. The feelings of isolation parents of challenging children face were compounded for me because Chrissy is also one of the estimated 30 to 40 per cent of people with learning difficulties, the cause of whose problems remains undiagnosed.

This book aims to blend facts with feelings. I hope, by writing it, to smooth the path for other parents in similar situations to my own. By sharing my experience and information I have gathered, I hope to dispel myths and help society to be better educated about challenging behaviour.

Acknowledgements

To my partner, Ian Alcock, for his encouragement with this project, and help with the technical stuff on the numerous occasions that I have fallen out with my computer. Most importantly, appreciation for his tireless love and support since he became Chrissy's stepdad.

To Ian's parents, Floss and Peter Alcock, for accepting Chrissy and her siblings as their own grandchildren.

To my mum, Jean Kirby, and sister, Sarah Catt – for their belief in me when I seemed to be the only one worrying about Chrissy's development. For their continuing patience with the problems that my family has experienced.

To friends, Elaine Payne and Olwen Vigart, for supporting me by boosting my flagging confidence over this creative endeavour, and for their affection for and interest in Chrissy. To other friends, Bev Tappin, Linda Popely, Carole Sealy and Dee Thomas, for providing a sympathetic ear at various times when the going has got tough. Also for sharing laughs and keeping me company on occasions when I let my hair down!

To Jeannine Bryans, a friend and professional foster carer, for her invaluable advice on managing disturbed behaviour in children.

To friends I have met through the years that have been interested in learning about the causes, treatment and effects of challenging behaviour instead of taking it at face value and being dismissive or judgemental.

To other mums of children with learning disabilities who have shared their experiences in order to help other parents cope, especially those I met through Contact '81, a parents' support group. Also, thanks to Vivien Cooper, another mum, who runs the Challenging Behaviour Foundation, for her information pack, for recommending professional contacts and for useful books that have contributed to this project.

Thanks to the professionals who have taken an interest in Chrissy and have helped her develop into the person she is now. These include staff at St Elizabeth's School (Much Hadham, Herts), Woodfield School, Collett School and Woolmer Drive respite services (in Hemel Hempstead).

I cannot name all the health and social work professionals who have helped Chrissy over the years. But I would like to give a special mention to Dr Janet Hislop, Linda Sayles (Chrissy's social worker), the nursing staff at St Elizabeth's School, and the tireless home care workers who have helped me in the school holidays, particularly Amber Jobson, Miriam Chaston, Nikki Upton and Lisa Francis, whom I now consider friends.

To my much-loved youngest daughter, Alex, for putting up with me tapping away at my computer when she has wanted my attention, and for her sweetness and affection – *most* of the time!

To Jamie, my son. Having a sibling with such very special needs robbed you of the childhood you deserved and made you, at times, doubt my love for you. If this book takes you one step further towards coming to terms with all that has happened to you, it will have been worth writing for that alone.

Finally, a thank you to Chrissy, my complicated, beautiful child, for providing me with the inspiration for this labour of love and helping me to grow as a person and examine my perspectives on life.

Introduction

So what exactly is 'challenging behaviour'? It is a label used to describe 'problem' behaviours shown by children and adults with a learning disability. The following definition of the term is widely used:

> ...behaviours of such intensity and frequency that the physical safety of the person or others is likely to be placed in jeopardy, or behaviour which is likely to seriously limit or delay access to and use of ordinary community services. (Emerson *et al.* 1987)

Overcoming severe challenging behaviour is no easy task. But reducing such behaviours will improve the individual's chances of reaching his or her maximum potential. Also, others will respond better to that individual. After all, who wants to interact with someone who lashes out or spits at them? Spitting and hitting are just two of the many and varied behaviours shown, which may also include:

- self-injurious behaviour, such as eye-poking, head-banging or biting own hands
- aggression to others, such as biting, kicking and hair pulling.
- destruction of property, such as breaking windows, throwing objects, stripping off, and ripping clothes
- sleep problems
- unacceptable verbal habits, such as swearing, constantly interrupting, saying inappropriate things in public and repetitive questions

- socially unacceptable habits, such as public masturbation, eating inedible objects (known as pica), and passing wind in public (or letting people know that someone else has!)
- hyperactivity
- inappropriate sexual behaviour (public masturbation) or inappropriate physical contact (such as hugging strangers)
- deliberate wetting or soiling.

These behaviours reduce the individuals' and their carers' quality of life and, if severe, can cause serious injuries (eye-poking can cause blindness, head-banging can cause brain damage and detached retinas).

Challenging behaviour is relatively common amongst people with learning disabilities. Recent British studies (e.g. Corbett, Murphy and Oliver 1987) indicate rates between 7 and 18 per cent. The behaviour of one in six people with learning disabilities is a major cause of stress for families and plays a key role in families' decisions to seek residential care. It is more common in people with particularly poor expressive language and social skills and additional sensory impairments. Therefore it follows that challenging behaviour is more frequent and severe at the lower end of the learning disability spectrum.

Challenging behaviour has many different and complex causes. Rarely is there one single cause in individual cases and the same behaviour may be exhibited for different reasons. For example, head-banging could mean: 'I'm hungry', 'I want attention', 'I do not want to do this' or 'My ear hurts'. Challenging behaviour often serves a purpose for the child or adult with learning disabilities. Ritualistic and stereotyped behaviours such as rocking and hand-flapping may reward the child by stimulating them when bored. Self-injury may trigger the release of morphine-like substances in the brain. Also, it is a guaranteed attention grabber. What adult can ignore a child hurting itself?

It helps if you think about toddlers without learning disabilities going through the 'terrible twos'. Before long, they develop other means to get their needs met. Some people with learning disabilities never develop enough communication and social skills to enable them to get what they want. The more demands put upon them the more they may display challenging behaviour in order to control what is going on around them or gain attention from carers. For example, if they are asked to help clear the table they may become agitated and have to be removed or restrained in order to calm them down. This effectively allows them to avoid the task. Transitions are particularly difficult for children with severe learning disabilities and challenging behaviour. Some children find it hard just to go from one room to another.

Many children who display challenging behaviours have additional limitations, such as epilepsy, autism and sensory impairment associated with, or as a result of, their conditions. These add to any sense of disorientation and confusion they may have about their world.

It is also worth considering biological or emotional causes, especially if the behaviour has worsened suddenly. Many children with learning disabilities are unable to locate their pain, so would not be able to indicate that their head ached or ear hurt. Emotional causes could range from a major upheaval, like a house move, to a change in routine, such as a different teacher at school.

Environmental factors should be taken into account too. When children without learning disabilities are exposed to social deprivation or abuse they also show disturbed behaviour.

Underlying psychiatric disorders may trigger challenging behaviour. A dual diagnosis of learning disability and mental illness is often delayed because psychiatric disorders, such as depression, may manifest themselves differently or be masked by the learning disabilities – so-called 'diagnostic overshadowing'.

Neurological disorders may also play a large part. For instance, when epilepsy is well controlled, behaviour can deteriorate. Also, imagine the confusion a child may feel after 'coming round' from an absence and missing a chunk of time. Subclinical seizure activity (a state of abnormal brain functioning) and anticonvulsants can also affect behaviour. When a child has both epilepsy and challenging behaviour, psychotropic medication may be used in conjunction with anticonvulsants. Unfortunately, some psychotropic medications lower seizure threshold. With the added complication that some children react adversely to certain medications, striking the right balance can be difficult.

Specific behaviours are known to be prevalent in certain genetic conditions. People with Smith–Magenis syndrome commonly suffer sleep problems and prolonged bouts of distress or outbursts. Destructiveness and a low frustration threshold are often noted in people with cri du chat syndrome. These observations have wider implications for the rest of us. The broader issue of genetically driven behaviours is the subject of much controversy; there is still much to discover as further advances are made in this field.

Whatever the causes of an individual's challenging behaviour, parents who understand why it occurs experience less stress. Most commonly, parents passively accept the behaviour, which leads to a higher likelihood of suffering stress-related conditions such as back pain, depression, anxiety and fatigue than parents who analyse the situation, make a plan of action, then follow it or ask someone for practical help.

Part 1

Early Years

CHAPTER I

Chrissy's Birth and Early Development

A tidal wave of love hit me the moment I saw Chrissy. She looked perfect with wide-open dark eyes, silky brown hair and unblemished skin. I understood why my mother had tried to fob me off about labour pains, claiming: 'The end result is worth it.' Only moments before, I could think of nothing but the intense pain. Yet the minute I held Chrissy I felt euphoric.

Chrissy did not need special care and she gave medical staff no cause for concern. Like many new mums I believed that if babies had no apparent problems at, or soon after, birth we were out of the woods. If learning disabilities are mentioned in baby books it is usually to describe how parents react to the bad news. Only rarely do books indicate that some conditions only become apparent as a child grows.

We had no family history of learning disability. My knowledge was confined to specific conditions like spina bifida, cerebral palsy or Down's syndrome. The words every mother dreads – 'I'm sorry, your baby's handicapped' – were never spoken at any time in Chrissy's life. I cannot help wishing they had been. At least we would have had a point from which to grieve.

Chrissy was our first baby. Once I moved in with her father, Tony, early in 1983 we started trying for a baby. I was already two months pregnant with her when my register office wedding to Tony took place in Hemel Hempstead on 10 September 1983. Tony, 31, was the middle son of Greek-Cypriot immigrants living in Edmonton. I was

22 and the middle child of middle-class parents whose family home was in Hemel Hempstead. The wedding buffet, held in a marquee in my mother's garden, was a resplendent mix of traditional Greek delicacies like dolmathakia latheres (stuffed grapevine leaves) and keftethes (meat patties) and English dishes like cold meat platters, sandwiches and quiche.

Four months into my pregnancy I gave up my full-time job as a secretary to concentrate on preparing for impending motherhood. Tony had exacting standards when it came to running a home and I strove, as an anxious young newly-wed, to prove that I was as good a homemaker as any traditional Greek-Cypriot wife. I had to learn from scratch; I did not even know how to boil an egg when we moved into our smart Mill Hill home.

Tony had his own company, selling and fitting security systems. He was on call and worked unpredictable hours. He introduced me to his colourful social life, which was intertwined with his work. I never knew whom he was going to bring home or take me to see next. He flew through life by the seat of his pants and was very gregarious. He made friends at every level of society: from tenants he chatted with as he connected entry phones outside their run-down council blocks, to a Nigerian prince he met as he fitted a sophisticated security system at his upmarket mansion.

I changed from the fun-loving party animal that blended easily into Tony's hedonistic lifestyle into someone who was happy to stay at home preparing for impending motherhood.

My pregnancy was uneventful. Apart from nausea and a bout of nasty headaches in the first three months, I was well. I gained the mandatory two stone, wore maternity smocks and baggy tracksuits, read babycare books and learnt to knit. I had fears in common with many mums-to-be at that time; more to do with bringing a baby into a world with the looming threat of nuclear war then having a handicapped child.

When I was ten days overdue doctors at Edgware Hospital brought me in and induced the baby. Despite attending antenatal classes, I was totally unprepared for the rigours of labour and birth. I was given a shave and an enema – completely old-fashioned (and many would say unnecessary) procedures. I had no contractions, so I was given a vaginal pessary. But nothing happened. I was hooked up to a drip and given Syntocinon to stimulate contractions. My waters were artificially broken and I had several painful internals to establish dilation of my uterus. I felt invaded and terrified, and wondered what the baby was going through.

The contractions hit me like a kick in the stomach. There was no gradual build-up, just immediate, excruciating cramps which went on for 16 hours. Pethidine and gas and air made me feel out of control, and rendered my breathing exercises useless. I kept drifting off between contractions and dreaming I was at home in bed, then, slam! I was brought back to earth as the pain of another contraction penetrated my fogged brain. Thankfully, an anaesthetist was available to give me an epidural when I could no longer bear the pains.

The midwife was busy and frequently left Tony alone with me to deal with other mums-to-be. At one point the baby's heart rate dropped dramatically on the monitor, but it picked up again fast enough for the midwife to allow my labour to continue without intervention.

As in most first births the second stage lasted a long time – between one and two hours. Chrissy was born at 9.45pm on 11 April 1984. She was quiet when she came out, and was whisked quickly off, out of my vision. It was at that point Tony phoned my mother to tell her she had a granddaughter, leaving her hovering anxiously by the phone for an update when he mentioned Chrissy had not made a sound. However, after having the mucus sucked out of her lungs, Chrissy appeared to be fine. Her Apgar scores started off low, but indicated a full recovery. It was the first time I had seen tears in Tony's eyes. He was very much the proud, doting father.

The night after Chrissy's birth, I woke up overwhelmed with joy at the sight of her sleeping in the perspex cot at the end of my hospital bed. I was bursting with pride – awed at the part I had played in creating something so perfect. Friends and family agreed that she was one of the most flawless and alert-looking newborns they had seen. We called her our 'air traffic controller' because her hands waved around energetically whenever she was awake.

We stayed in hospital for six days, as was the norm for most new mums then. I used that time to try to establish regular feeds, and to learn how to bath and care for my baby. I could not understand all the fuss about breastfeeding – Chrissy barely tickled my nipple as she sucked. A nurse who helped me remarked that Chrissy looked premature, despite her healthy birth weight of seven pounds six ounces.

I had read all the textbooks, including the one my own mother had used, Dr Benjamin Spock's babycare 'bible' (the one he wrote before he retracted most of what he had preached!). But I had no practical experience because I had not been around babies much. Chrissy did not feed well and she had jaundice, not enough for light treatment, but for longer than the other babies on our ward. Most newborns lose weight after the birth and before the mother's milk comes in. Chrissy's weight dropped to under six pounds. Medical staff kept an eye on her but did not seem unduly concerned.

Chrissy was a placid, sleepy baby once we got home. Failure to thrive was the first sign anything was wrong. She vomited up most of her feeds but the midwife said, after checking it was not projectile, that sickness was common in young babies. She advised me to wake her for feeds.

'The head control's poor,' commented my health visitor on a routine visit when Chrissy was two months old. 'I'll refer her to a paediatrician, though it's probably nothing to worry about.'

I had no idea how significant these signs were. I just gradually became aware that something was not quite right. Because she was our first child I did not know what to expect and, therefore, felt a lot of guilt when I questioned whether she was 'normal'.

The usual milestones took an awful lot of prompting to develop and they came late. I wonder now, if I had known that Chrissy had learning disabilities, would I have tried so hard to make her reach out for objects, sit up, crawl and walk? Would I have been more patient over her slow eating? In short, would I have enjoyed her more if I had expected less? In some ways, having higher expectations than Chrissy could meet was an advantage because it meant that I did all I could to urge her on. In other ways, having high expectations was a curse because it led to a lot of frustration and disappointment.

Mealtimes were hard going. On my health visitor's advice I started supplementing feeds before Chrissy was two months old. As the weaning stage progressed I did everything wrong. I lovingly prepared special purees, like lentil broth and home-made casseroles, then felt furious when Chrissy either refused them or heaved them up. The elderly man next door popped his head over the fence once and admonished me for shouting at Chrissy when she would not eat her meal. I still feel ashamed at the anger I felt (and expressed!) over her refusing food. My mother said that my brother, who had a heart condition, was the same. She used to get beside herself too. What is it about babies and food? Do we feel personally slighted when we cannot nourish them? I suspect it is about our own sense of failure.

It was not all doom and gloom. Chrissy was responsive and cheerful. The summer after I had her was glorious – the hottest April for a hundred years. One baby is very portable, and she was so adaptable I could take her anywhere. She would just sit in her baby chair, cooing, smiling and watching the world go by.

'If my baby turns out like yours I'll be over the moon,' said a friend who was pregnant with her first.

Little did I know how poignant that throwaway remark would prove to be.

There were other mums with young families around me. I could not help comparing Chrissy with their babies. A neighbour's baby was twice the size of Chrissy at the same age. If you lifted her under her arms she came up in one piece. Chrissy flopped all over the place, and I still had to support her head. She did not sit until she was eight-and-a-half months old. Then she did it only once, before adding the skill permanently to her repertoire at ten months. She crawled at 12 months and walked at 22 months. But the greatest delay was her language development.

At nine months Chrissy was assessed by a speech therapist, an occupational therapist and a physiotherapist. The physiotherapist gave us strength-building exercises to do with her. Chrissy was still very floppy and barely sitting up. We were lucky, living in Edgware (we moved there from Mill Hill in 1985), because those three therapies were readily available. It was a puzzling time. When pressed, the therapists, my GP and health visitor said Chrissy had developmental delay. To me, the implications of that term were that she might catch up. When I asked if that was possible I was told that no one knew what the future held for Chrissy. But catching up was a possibility.

Some parents would rather not be told in stark terms that their child would probably grow up with learning disabilities. They have a natural tendency to minimise the problem or deny anything is wrong when they first realise that their child is different. But I wanted honesty. I needed confirmation of the fears that sneaked up on me while I lay awake in bed. When I voiced those fears to Tony, at first he dismissed them.

'It's as if you *want* her to be handicapped,' he accused.

Then, when he could deny it no longer, it was: 'Well, it must have come from your family because there's nothing like this in ours.'

Our friends, Monica and Stefan, came round one day with their little girl who, at nine months, was the same age as Chrissy. Their daughter was into everything, whereas Chrissy was quite happy lying on the carpet. When I spoke to them on the phone soon afterwards I mentioned my concerns about Chrissy's development.

'Well, do you still leave her on the floor without stimulating her?' Stefan demanded.

I was lost for words. Comments like that you never forget. They only added to the burden of guilt I already felt about Chrissy's lack of progress.

As with most first babies, Chrissy *did not* lack stimulation. My family were captivated by her. Mum and I spent hours encouraging progress by waving things, like plant leaves and baby rattles, at Chrissy. Every tentative movement in their general direction would elicit great excitement from us. Later, we surrounded her with cushions, propped her up, then moved them away (staying close by to catch her!) in the hope that she would stay sitting. Chrissy loved fruit-flavoured fromage frais and, when she was between 16 and 24 months, we would lean her against the wall and tantalise her with the little pot in the hope she would take a few steps towards it.

Most toys we bought were geared up to Chrissy's next developmental stage; we could also borrow toys from our local toy library. The occupational therapist was a useful source of information. She taught us the sequential stages that babies go through, like posting and screwing things on. Rather than discarding toys that were ignored, we hid them, then brought them out at a later date to find Chrissy ready to enjoy them.

At one stage, in trying to develop Chrissy's pincer grip, we sat her in the garden with a large pot of lentils. They ended up all over the grass, and stuck to Chrissy's bottom, much to her consternation! Chrissy preferred toys that responded noisily to her touch, like the Fisher-Price Activity Centre and her jack-in-the-box. She also liked simple musical instruments, such as bells and trumpets. Like the stereotypical learning disabled child, she loved music and had a great sense of rhythm. Chrissy's fine motor development was ahead of the rest of her development. She became quite proficient at jigsaw puzzles and shape sorting by posting shapes in appropriate holes. She was able to hold a pencil properly and draw almost age-appropriately.

As already mentioned, speech and language development was the greatest cause for concern. Chrissy went through every stage of development, but later than other babies. The only one she missed was the mouthing stage. The speech therapist said that this was very significant in view of her speech delay. We had to encourage her to use her mouth as much as possible. Chewing food, blowing bubbles, sucking straws, and making and copying sounds would all help her develop speech.

Despite the concern over Chrissy's developmental delay, she had all her vaccinations, including whooping cough. I did not know then that if there is any suspicion of neurological problems it was inadvisable to give the whooping cough vaccine; and no one told me of this. Concern over Chrissy's weight gain had been expressed in her medical notes on 15 May 1984 when she was a month old. When she was almost three months old, 'failure to thrive', 'poor head control' and 'acts like a six-week-old baby' were written by my GP in

Chrissy's notes. Yet the first triple vaccine was given on 6 July 1984. The trouble was, this put us in a catch-22 situation. Because Chrissy had obvious signs of developmental delay before the vaccinations, it made it hard to say (or for a court to judge) whether the vaccine had added to that damage and, if so, by how much. For many years I was to latch on to everything from the whooping cough vaccine to the protracted birth as a possible cause for Chrissy's problems.

Ten days after Chrissy's third whooping cough vaccination she had her first febrile convulsion.

CHAPTER 2

Why Won't Anyone Tell Us What's Wrong?

Christina, a female relative from Cyprus, was spending the day with us when Chrissy had her first convulsion. Chrissy, at 10 months, was still tiny, and looked about half her chronological age. We had been to Wembley market, and Chrissy was fretful and feverish. I thought the hot summer weather had contributed to her temperature. We gave her Calpol, but when Christina tried to give her a bottle of juice while Chrissy was lying on her lap, Chrissy's eyes suddenly rolled up in her head, she went rigid and started turning blue. Luckily, Christina had witnessed a febrile convulsion before and knew immediately what it was. Nonetheless, I felt utter panic at the sight of Chrissy's blue-tinged skin, frothing mouth and fixed stare. I thought she was dying.

With shaking fingers I dialled an ambulance and we were rushed to Edgware Hospital's casualty department where Chrissy proceeded to have two further fits. They could not have lasted longer than a minute or so, but it seemed like ages. In between fits Chrissy was lethargic and shivery, and made a strange droning sound.

Doctors confirmed that Chrissy was having febrile convulsions. They explained that they were quite common in children under three because the immature brain is easily irritated by a high temperature. They assured me that very few children go on to develop epilepsy. However, no cause was found for the fever and, because of additional concerns over Chrissy's developmental delay, cerebral investigations were arranged.

I could not help wondering whether there was a connection between the fits and the third whooping cough vaccine Chrissy had been given ten days before. I had not noticed any reaction after the previous vaccinations, but then I had not been looking for one. I doubt that I would have picked up on a more subtle reaction, like irritability and a runny nose; I was used to Chrissy being ill from recurrent ear, chest and throat infections.

Chrissy stayed in hospital for three days. Our paediatrician barely communicated with me as he examined her. I was bursting with questions and full of anxiety. Chrissy had been able to move around in a baby walker, but during her stay in hospital she regressed and became floppy and unsteady in the walker.

'Is she going to be mentally handicapped?' I asked our paediatrician when he finished examining Chrissy.

'There's a possibility she could be retarded, yes,' he remarked briskly.

Before I could ask him to elaborate he turned on his heel, and left to continue his ward round. The world suddenly seemed a cold and frightening place.

On the evening after we returned home our GP came to see us. She sat down with us in the living room and murmured, 'I'm so sorry.'

'What for?' I asked.

There was an awkward silence. Despite her gentle manner, I was immediately alert and on the defensive. Did she know something I did not? Perhaps one of the tests had shown something. I racked my brain to remember which tests Chrissy had been given recently. Our GP mentioned Chrissy being in hospital and the developmental delay. I felt that she had come round specifically to commiserate with us about some news she thought had been broken to us in hospital. But she did not come to the point.

'Do you know something we don't?' I challenged her. Our GP assured me that she did not.

I was desperate for a medical professional to endorse my fears about Chrissy having learning disabilities. If our GP had not come to tell us the bad news, what was the purpose of her visit? It seemed as though she had come to comfort us, but for what exactly?

That feeling of no one telling us what they thought about Chrissy persisted throughout early communications with health professionals. Now I can understand their reluctance to commit themselves. What if they got it wrong? I could have been worried needlessly. And maybe they see other children similarly delayed to Chrissy who catch up.

I felt even more confused after the GP's visit, and peeked at Chrissy's medical notes every time she was rushed into hospital with convulsions. I never found anything much other than a registrar's comments: 'Mother worried as usual. Asked if daughter was mentally handicapped. Told her I did not know.'

Chrissy had to be admitted about twice a year with convulsions that, before she was two, developed into non-febrile ones. They usually occurred in runs and had to be stopped with medication. She was put on an anticonvulsant, phenytoin, though at that time her EEG showed no abnormalities. Once, Chrissy had a particularly bad run of fits at her grandparents' home in Edmonton, so we took her straight to the nearest casualty unit, The University College Hospital (UCH), London.

We were feeling dissatisfied at the lack of progress made in helping Chrissy at Edgware, so we asked to be transferred to the UCH. Each time we saw another doctor I felt a surge of hope that they would spot something the others had not. In my mind I suppose the diagnosis was tied up with a cure. If we found out what was wrong, we could make it better. My quest for a diagnosis bordered on the obsessive. We fell into the classic trap of traipsing around to different specialists. It kept hope alive. Someone, somewhere, must be able to help us. The trouble is, once you suspect that there is something wrong with your child you are immediately in the throes of taking action. It leaves you with no time to process your emotions.

Chrissy had a battery of tests, including a brain scan in March 1985, which showed mild generalised cerebral atrophy or under-development. Her new paediatrician dismissed it as insignificant.

'We would expect many children without developmental delay to show something like this on a scan,' he said. 'By the same token, some children with profound learning disabilities show nothing on their brain scans.'

I felt disappointed that nothing more concrete had been found. It had taken an hour and a half by train to get Chrissy to the hospital. We had waited for over an hour with Chrissy in a terrible tantrum. I dreaded the train journey home.

'Feel the lumps all over her head,' I exploded tearfully at the poor receptionist in the hospital waiting area. 'This is what she does at home and no one can tell me why!'

The train journey home was a nightmare. It was rush hour, and Chrissy carried on screaming and trying to bash her head everywhere. I restrained her silently while the other passengers looked on equally silently (and some disapprovingly).

Typically, I latched on to the cerebral atrophy. My father, who had premature Alzheimer's disease, was told that his brain scan showed cerebral atrophy too. He also developed epilepsy.

In the summer of 1985, during the early stages of his illness, we went to the Lake District, just mum, dad, Chrissy and I. We stayed in a small guesthouse in Cockermouth. I was pregnant with my second child and quite content to spend the evenings drinking cocoa and playing Scrabble with mum. We spent the days sightseeing, shopping, taking in the majesty of the fells and eating delicious lunches out. All the driving around lulled Chrissy to sleep. She was on the anticonvulsant phenytoin, and I wondered if it was sedating her too much and therefore hindering her development.

I do not think anyone at the guesthouse realised that there was anything wrong with Chrissy. She was at her most cute and 'squidgy' stage. As the only young child there she captivated the other guests.

'Just look at those shoe button eyes,' an American guest exclaimed every time he spotted her.

Chrissy is loose-jointed and her favourite trick was to put her foot up to her ear and, with our encouragement ('talk on the telephone, Chrissy'), she would babble gobbledegook into her heel! She has a talent for mimicry, and did a fair imitation of my voice even then without being able to actually form the words.

I had been so wrapped up in Chrissy's problems I had not noticed how dad had declined and the stress it was putting mum under. Dad left taps on and wandered around in the night. He occasionally wandered off during the day too, and was involved in a car accident that put him in hospital. Physically, although not violent, he was becoming harder to manage. He was a big man, and mum had to deal with his most basic needs; but it was her emotional state that was most affected. She was in no position to support me, although she tried. It was a difficult time for us all, watching dad deteriorate and, at the same time, realising the extent of Chrissy's problems.

Dad and Chrissy developed an instinctive rapport. Dad was gentle and affectionate with her, and she did not make a fuss at his bumbling attempts to hold her and talk to her. All the children called him 'dad-dad' after my children's early attempts at the word 'grandad'. In the latter stages of dad's illness Chrissy would sing 'Baa-baa Black Sheep' to him and he would smile sweetly.

I got further 'confirmation' of Chrissy's learning disabilities near the end of my confinement. I had felt less foetal movement and was taken in to the UCH for monitoring. As I was strapped to the heart monitor I spotted a piece of paper with my details on it. It read: '1 + 0 mentally handicapped.' I did not take in the rest. Someone at the UCH had obviously taken notes when my GP rang to get me monitored. There it was in black and white. So doctors *did* think Chrissy was 'mentally handicapped'. I had latched on to something insignificant again, someone's hastily scribbled notes. It was a turning point though.

Thereafter, when I spoke about Chrissy to medical professionals, I said she was mentally handicapped, although I know the term has since been replaced by 'learning difficulties' or 'special needs'. I bandied the words 'mental handicap' around quite a bit after reading that note. They shut people up who remarked on Chrissy's behaviour. One such person was the orthoptist we saw at our local health centre in Hemel Hempstead after our move from Edgware to Bovingdon, Hertfordshire. Chrissy was being seen for an alternating squint. As usual, she would not co-operate; she loathed medical procedures.

'What on earth have you done to her to make her behave like this?' the orthoptist snapped.

'She's mentally handicapped,' I said grimly. 'She doesn't understand why you're shining lights into her eyes.'

'Oh, sorry,' she said grudgingly. 'She doesn't look it.'

Chrissy *did not* look it then. She was just very small for her age, which made it easier for people to accept her tantrums. Few people expect very young children to behave impeccably.

My son, Jamie, was born on 4 December 1985 at the UCH, three weeks after his due date. I had held on, adamant about not being induced again. I felt well and was not worried about having another baby like Chrissy. This was because I was still unsure about the extent of Chrissy's learning disabilities and I blamed the birth and the whooping cough vaccine rather than anything genetic. My second labour was much easier and shorter than my first and Jamie was healthy, weighing a strapping eight pounds six ounces. Because he was so overdue, his skull bones had hardened, and he was born with a cephalhaematoma, a protrusion on one side of his head. I felt very protective towards him when people asked: 'What's that on his head?' Nurses assured me that it would not do Jamie any harm, and it went down within about six weeks after the birth.

It was even more of a struggle with two little ones. Chrissy often ended up in hospital because her seizures occurred in runs and needed medical intervention to stop them. I had to find childcare for Jamie during our stays in hospital. Mum had no choice but to oblige, often at a moment's notice. It was tough for her with dad to look after as well.

Chrissy's general health was poor. She kept having bouts of diarrhoea and was also being seen regularly about her ears. She had glue ear and her eardrums kept perforating. For a time I wondered if that was what was causing her outbursts. I am certain that the pain was one of the contributors. As I wrote in the introduction, there can be many causes for specific problem behaviours.

In June 1986 Chrissy had her first operation to insert grommets. Subsequently, she had further operations to fit grommets, and later, T-tubes (grommets that are more firmly anchored in the ears than the grommets used for glue ear). Her speech delay was not helped by the glue ear problem. Neither were her fits. The high temperatures brought on by ear infections irritated her immature brain.

Chrissy's fits were not controlled by phenytoin. I still panicked as late as Chrissy's second birthday when she had a fit because I felt I had to do something, intervene somehow. This feeling of needing to 'stop' Chrissy's fits was exacerbated by an occasion in Edgware when Chrissy choked on some food and started convulsing as she was eating. I rushed out into the street.

'Someone help me! My baby's stopped breathing!' I screamed.

Most of my neighbours were Jewish and, as it was Saturday lunchtime, they were returning from the nearby synagogue. Without hesitation, one of the passers-by I appealed to stuck his hand down Chrissy's throat and withdrew the blockage. In my panic I had locked myself out, and I used a neighbour's phone to call an ambulance. Our saviour melted into the crowd and I never saw him again to thank him properly.

Once I got used to the convulsions, understood that each one was self-limiting and that because she was unconscious Chrissy was not suffering in them, I stopped throwing her at neighbours to deal with. My fear had been born of ignorance. I got the information and therefore the reassurance I needed, not from medical professionals, but from the local library. Later I discovered and used organisations like the British Epilepsy Association and the National Society for Epilepsy. I also asked doctors, therapists and teachers about sources of information, and approached the special educational department at my local university.

Seeking information from different sources helps you to make decisions about what is best for your child and enables you to play an active role in your learning disabled child's life, rather than accepting advice passively. Once I became informed about epilepsy, Chrissy's prolonged screaming bouts worried me more than the fits. At least I knew what the fits were.

Although Chrissy was an exceptionally placid baby, when she was as young as one month old I approached my GP about periods of inconsolable screaming mid-morning and evening. It was put down to colic even though she did not curl her knees up into her tummy. On the contrary, she stiffened up, and arched her back. The screaming would start without any apparent trigger. When Chrissy was three months old my friend, Bev, was holding her when Chrissy suddenly threw herself backwards and started screaming. Bev nearly dropped her; it was that sudden.

Bev's son, Marc, was the same age as Chrissy. When he was eighteen months old, I remember being startled when he responded to me mumbling to myself 'where's the tissues?' while visiting his home one day. He toddled off to pick up a box of tissues and deposited them on my lap. He was a genius; so advanced! Of course, Marc was just exhibiting the usual comprehension skills for a child his age. Just as I could not help comparing Chrissy to her peers, people had noticed that Chrissy was not behaving normally. Much later, Bev reminded me of that incident when Chrissy had arched backwards in her arms, and how odd she had thought it.

However, some babies frequently appear distressed without good reason, so I did not become overly concerned until Chrissy was more mobile and able to throw herself around in tantrums. The tantrums had a reciprocal relationship with the fits. I much preferred the fits!

Chrissy only had one or two major seizures a month. The screaming outbursts came in clusters. Chrissy could have three or four outbursts in one day, each one lasting up to three hours, but usually lasting about thirty minutes to an hour. The first outburst in a run was usually the most violent and prolonged, or maybe it felt that way because we had not become acclimatised to them! Because Chrissy was placid, the outbursts seemed more marked.

The outbursts became as much a part of Chrissy as her epilepsy. As a family we developed our own little phrases to describe something outside the realms of our experience, and to try and inject some humour into it all. Because the outbursts often started at around four o'clock we called them her 'four o'clock flips'. They seemed to appear around sleep, either on waking from her afternoon nap or when she was over-tired. Chrissy appeared to be in great pain or tormented by something. She got what I called her 'wild bull's eyes' and thrashed around the room, banging her head off every hard surface she could find. She tried to throw herself down the stairs and bit us when we tried to restrain her. And, when she was barely two, she inadvertently head-butted a doctor who was trying to examine her, knocking her glasses off and flustering her.

You need to deal with these outbursts from start to finish to understand how bizarre they are. I described them to one doctor as like 'something out of *The Exorcist*, as if she's possessed'. I felt foolish, but how do you describe something that you do not understand yourself? In them Chrissy appeared terrified by her own lack of control, but powerless to come out of that state. She looked like she was in agony.

I could not believe that Chrissy was the only person who had suffered like this. Surely someone must be able to pinpoint and treat the cause of her torment? Or maybe one day Chrissy would develop the necessary communication skills to be able to tell me what she was feeling.

CHAPTER 3

Trying to Cope

We moved twice before Chrissy was three. Our second move was to Bovingdon, Hertfordshire, nearer to where my parents lived.

I made Chrissy a chocolate 'Care Bear' cake for her third birthday party. She loved one of the *Care Bear* videos and watched it over and over again. As with many new interests she developed or skills she learned, she became obsessive about them. Not content to sit and watch them, she preferred to rewind and fast-forward the tape continually. Then she would become agitated, a state that often led to screaming outbursts.

Unfortunately, because of the dramatic variations in Chrissy's behaviour, she did not always 'perform' when I wanted her to. I had been lucky with all my health visitors, and I had a particularly helpful one in Bovingdon. I taped one of the outbursts for her and she listened to it attentively, and confessed that she did not have a clue what it was.

My health visitor arranged an appointment with my GP, who, I was told, had a special interest in paediatrics. He allowed me a lot of time but did not appear to listen to what I was saying. I left the appointment feeling patronised and misunderstood. I was not surprised to read his comments in Chrissy's medical notes: 'Mum says is miserable at home. Throughout this long consultation Christina was happy and playing in the room. Looks well. Further reassurance.' Chrissy was not miserable at home *most* of the time. It was the wide variations in her behaviour that I was trying to highlight. I wish I had taken someone with me. Meetings with professionals can be very tense.

There are various other ways in which having someone there with you can help. Having another person with you can defuse tense situations. Another person can take notes and help you clarify issues raised. Afterwards you can discuss and share observations about the meeting, and the other person can help you work out a plan of action if you need to pursue specific issues.

Hospital visits are particularly time-consuming and tiring. You need to be prepared for appointments as far as possible, taking a pen and paper for making notes, and packing baby wipes, toys, drinks and foods. Allow yourself plenty of time by ensuring that you do not have to rush back for anything and, if necessary, making sure that siblings are picked up from school.

My GP's attitude had added to my guilt feelings. Were Chrissy's outbursts something I was doing wrong? Were they not as bad as I imagined them to be? Chrissy could be so sweet and amenable, especially during periods when she was having fits, that I would be lulled into a false sense of security. How easily we bury ongoing, unpleasant issues in our lives so that we can remain in our comfort zones! As soon as something better comes along we have that lovely quality of being able to forget what is bad. I doubted my own perceptions. When the outbursts started again I would feel stupid. Anyone could see that they were extremely disturbing and needed addressing. How could I have thought otherwise?

I felt powerless because nothing I did helped Chrissy and nobody had any idea why the outbursts occurred. I got the impression that medical professionals took them no more seriously than toddler tantrums.

An EEG done when Chrissy was three showed 'generalised epileptiform activity'. It was the first test that showed something conclusive, and I felt spookily comforted by that! My growing need to gain affirmation from the medical professionals about Chrissy's problems led to arguments with Tony. He did not want to discuss the future and felt I was 'downing' Chrissy by discussing her problems.

'I just want my gut feelings about Chrissy validated,' I tried to explain. 'Then I'd feel I could move on and try to help her.'

Chrissy started attending a local opportunity group, a weekly playgroup for pre-school children with and without learning disabilities. I got my hands on a book about different syndromes there and pored over it, pouncing on any syndromes that Chrissy might fit the bill for! At that time I thought I was the only parent whose child had no diagnosis.

Despite having moved nearer to my parents' home, I was finding it far tougher to cope with two little ones than I'd imagined. When Jamie was a baby I would breastfeed him while spoon-feeding Chrissy in her high chair. They were in nappies at the same time for more than two years. I was eventually able to get free nappies for Chrissy through the medical supplies department at my local council.

There was nothing wrong with the rate of Jamie's development. I called Jamie 'tortoise' when he was a tiny baby because if I laid him on his front he would lift his head up and gaze around the room. Jamie was physically stronger than the average baby his age. But I was also in awe of what babies do naturally. The children went through a 'twin' stage where they were the same height and at the same level developmentally. People were amazed when I told them that there were nineteen months between them.

I pushed them round in one of those ridiculously wide double buggies. Once, when I was trying to put the buggy up outside the opportunity group's venue, the children ran in opposite directions. It was a fairly busy street, and I did not know which one to go after. A group of youths stood by and roared at my plight.

'Don't just laugh. Get one of them!' I panted indignantly as I chased Jamie (because he could run the fastest!).

Looking back they were a comical pair; but, sadly, for much of the time my sense of humour got lost in all the drudgery, as it does for many mums of toddlers. I loved both my children dearly; they were deliciously edible, funny and affectionate. But that did not make daily management any easier.

Jamie spoke early and soon overtook Chrissy, developmentally and in size. But as a baby, he was as fractious and fidgety as Chrissy had been placid. Nothing I did pacified him. He did not settle at the breast and wriggled uncomfortably when I tried to cuddle him. Yet he screamed every time I put him down. He was also hypersensitive – the slightest sound made him jump out of his skin and dissolve into heartrending sobs. Maybe Jamie seemed demanding because Chrissy had been so peaceful. Even when he was born, he came out screaming! Tony had been restless and impulsive too, nor had I been an easy child. (My mother said that I had not settled at the breast either.) Jamie may have inherited those characteristics.

I was embarrassed about seeking medical advice for Jamie's persistent crying and irritability and wondered if medical professionals would label me a 'problem parent'. But life was a constant round of sleepless nights and exhausting days. I needed help. I had the impression that doctors thought my perceptions of my children's behaviour were distorted. Maybe it was the way I communicated my difficulties to them. I left after each appointment feeling even more that it was my fault. What was I doing wrong?

Medical professionals blamed Jamie's persistent crying on his being around Chrissy's challenging behaviour. He also had a constantly runny nose; one doctor suggested that it was due to him being a 'winter baby'!

I do not doubt that Chrissy's behaviour, genetics and the declining state of my marriage were contributory factors to Jamie's irritability, but I felt that there was something else that made Jamie hard to pacify, maybe food intolerances. He often seemed uncomfortable and colicky. Because on examination he appeared healthy, I felt that my concerns were dismissed. As he grew older I wondered about ADHD (attention deficit hyperactivity disorder), then known simply as hyperactivity. But one paediatrician I mentioned it to said that it was extremely rare, and only found in some children with additional severe handicaps.

Without wanting to marginalise the effects of environment on children's behaviour, it is worth mentioning here about the influence of difficult or irritable behaviour on parental functioning (Crockenberg 1981). Some babies are born more difficult than others. Just endorsing the parent's experience of her child may alleviate the sense that it is only her mishandling of the child that is causing the problem. This may lower the incidence of maternal depression, which can further worsen a child's behaviour. I mentioned the importance of early intervention in the introduction. There is less likelihood of longer-term behavioural difficulties in the child if healthcare professionals could work with parents to devise management strategies for difficult infant behaviour.

A recent report claims that one in six babies are born difficult (Murray *et al.* 1996). Research indicates that having an irritable baby makes mothers four times more likely to have postnatal depression. This can damage early bonding between mother and baby, and lead to long-term behaviour problems for the child. Support from friends and family is particularly important for such mothers. The reasons behind babies being born difficult are unclear. Social class does not appear to make a difference. Suggested causes are viral infections or diet (a contributory factor in colic, which makes babies more irritable).

As Jamie grew, his boisterousness and excitability bothered Chrissy. She needed her own space. If Jamie bumped into her or accidentally hurt her she would hurt herself too. It was the same if I smacked her or she knocked herself on something. She would smack herself wherever she had been hurt and get really agitated. Smacking either child was futile. That is not to say that I never did it. Sometimes I could not help myself!

For Jamie, having a disabled sibling was not much fun. We took many cute photos of them holding hands and sitting together at their 'twin' stage but in truth they rarely played together. Chrissy did not interact with her peer group then, and relied very much on adults to keep her amused.

She knew exactly how to wind Jamie up. She learned from an early age how to annoy people of all ages. One day, when Chrissy was about five and Jamie three, I heard this awful screeching coming from the kitchen. My heart pounding, I rushed to investigate and saw Jamie pinned, red-faced, up against the wall by nothing more than his own indignation as Chrissy repeated his name – 'Jamie, Jamie!' – with different intonations. It was as if she had a high-pressure hose turned on him. Chrissy was grinning wickedly all over her face, absolutely delighted.

If their behaviour got out of control I let them cry it out in a cot or playpen, and went off somewhere out of earshot. But when they got bigger this was not possible. I am a great believer in 'time out' but I did not appreciate the destruction of property that went along with leaving my children to vent their anger in another room. (This was more applicable to Chrissy, who was more destructive than Jamie.) So, weather permitting, I would let them have their tantrums in the garden. God knows what my neighbours thought!

It is easy for others to judge a situation at face value when they have not experienced anything similar. A friend with four children, two that have ADHD and one that has a learning disability, explained how people criticise her as a parent:

> They say things like: 'I wouldn't let my child do that.' But if a child constantly puts you up against it you have to relax some of your ideals and prioritise which behaviours you deal with. To outsiders it may look as though you're letting them get away with too much, but to pick them up over every misdemeanour only heightens their sense of being 'bad' and worsens your relationship with them.

Children with behaviour problems, with and without learning disabilities, have problems with self-image; and being punitive and confrontational is more likely to intensify the behaviour than change it. Often while you are addressing one behaviour, another needs addressing immediately afterwards or even at the same time! A friend with grown-up children gave her reaction to a scenario I put to her regarding a challenging child answering back. Without hesitation she said: 'I'd give her a good hiding.'

Annoyingly, her daughters are a credit to her and she still wallops them now if they speak out of turn! Of course that has strengthened her view that physical punishment works. My view is that she has just been lucky. I am not one of the vehement anti-smacking brigade, but for my children it has only ever intensified their bad behaviour.

Another bugbear is people who say: 'She was fine with me.' There is nothing more demoralising! Children tend to behave better with people outside the immediate family, especially those they do not know well. They can often sustain good behaviour for short periods of time.

A parent of a child with Tourette's syndrome (a condition characterised by multiple tics and obscene speech) told me how she felt when her son's teacher said that he was not particularly difficult at school.

'He comes home and unleashes all the pent-up tics and hyperactivity on the family,' she said. 'When I asked for support at home the implication was that I was the only one who had a problem with him.'

Chrissy's behaviour was as much of a problem with professional carers and teachers as at home. She had no inhibitions so was never on her 'best' behaviour for anyone!

What makes challenging behaviour so hard for parents is not just the physical and mental strain, but also the conflicting emotions. Love, pity, guilt, anger and despair are only a few of them. Nothing Chrissy did diminished my love for her. Watching her in bed asleep I felt torn in two. More than anyone, I saw the delightful core self underneath the behaviour.

At five years old Chrissy still needed lots of help with eating. She hated any food with lumps in or food she had to chew. She was obsessive about what she ate. Petit suisse was still her favourite, as were mushed up Weetabix and anything else wheat- or dairy-based. She could sit for hours before eating one mouthful but would scream in protest if I tried to remove her food before she was ready.

As I mentioned previously, eating problems often go hand in hand with delayed language development. When Chrissy was nearly three we saw a speech therapist at our local health centre. There was a long wait for the appointment and we were told speech therapy services were thin on the ground in our area. At this point we appreciated the various therapies and home visits that we had been given in Edgware. It was our first experience of the NHS lottery, where provision of certain services depends on your postcode.

At the age of five Chrissy's speech and language were still a long way behind. She had about a dozen words and could only follow instructions at a one-word level. The speech therapist was the only person to mention the autistic spectrum because Chrissy had fixed, repetitive phrases, such as 'what's that?' and 'gimme'. However, the speech therapist noted that Chrissy had symbolic play (she pretended to feed a large doll) and explored her environment. She suggested that when I talk to Chrissy I keep the language level simple and try to encourage chewing.

I had already asked about autism and been told by Chrissy's doctor that autistic children do not speak, and that therefore Chrissy could not possibly be autistic. I now know that to be utter rubbish. No wonder many children with autism go undiagnosed for years. Medical professionals familiar with autism later discounted it after observing Chrissy closely. One specialist even described Chrissy as 'unautistic', whatever that means!

We paid privately to have Chrissy's hearing checked and were told it was normal. NHS hearing checks had revealed nothing. The NHS tests involved Chrissy having to place a peg in a hole each time she heard a sound through earphones, but she could not understand what was being asked of her. Years later, when she was able to co-operate with the tests, I discovered that she had severe nerve deafness in her left ear, and reduced hearing ability in her right. No doubt the glue ear and frequent eardrum perforations also contributed to Chrissy's hearing loss.

So many tests were done on Chrissy during hospital admissions (CT scans, an MRI scan, numerous EEGs, chromosome testing, as well as routine ones like thyroid/liver function tests and blood levels). They were all normal apart from some of the EEGs that confirmed what we already knew – that Chrissy had epilepsy. The epilepsy was idiopathic, and no focus was found.

If conventional medicine could not help maybe alternative medicine could. My faith in conventional medicine had been severely shaken. When it came to health care I had taken so much for granted, believing that doctors had all the answers. But then I had only known about conventional ailments. I did not know which way to turn.

I tried various alternative therapies. One such was cranial osteopathy; Chrissy hated her head being touched so that was a no-go. I gathered information on other therapies, such as high doses of certain vitamins, homeopathy and environmental medicine. I never pursued any of those avenues because I thought it would be very hit or miss as we did not know what was wrong with Chrissy. Also she appeared to feel threatened by even the most non-intrusive medical examinations. Even massage seemed painful for her. Drying her after a bath made her moan and groan as if she had sensitive skin; yet a large bruise or red-raw fingers (where she had picked the nail away) did not bother her. Once she reached the age of about twelve she allowed and enjoyed people massaging her and playing with her hair.

When in 1988 I discovered I was pregnant with my third child I had mixed feelings. Although Tony was fine when I broke the news, I felt foolish about letting it happen. I could barely cope with the children I already had. But I longed for a healthy little girl. (Though I had no grounds to assume my third child would be female.) Maybe I wanted to duplicate my relationship with my mum, which had become a great source of pleasure now that she was a grandmother to my children. It was obvious by now that Chrissy would not be capable of having children. Also the idea of abortion was abhorrent to me, having already brought two much-loved children into the world. I was comforted by the knowledge that, when the baby was due, Jamie would be three, and at play school, and Chrissy would be nearly five and at full-time school.

However, I felt increasingly uneasy about my marriage. To out-siders, I had everything. A friend said to me recently: 'God, I envied you then. But you seemed to take it all for granted.'

My home was immaculate, and we gave lavish dinner parties. We were a typical eighties couple, living beyond our means with a large mortgage, a swimming pool in the back garden, and a succession of flash cars (Tony's passion). I had a different car every few months. Incredulous friends accused 'You don't know how lucky you are' when they noticed my dead eyes as they expressed envy at the latest one – a red Mercedes Sports.

Tony was self-employed and I had no idea that we were sinking into debt because he dealt with the bills. He was often moody and would snap 'It doesn't grow on trees' when I asked for money to go food shopping. Then he would come home with something extravagant like a new hi-fi system. If I asked questions, he would swear blind that a client gave it to him instead of wages. I admired his ability to barter. It was amazing how he always seemed to get such a good deal! He was far from mean with money, but he had different priorities from mine.

Our lives were diverging on different paths. We had little in common any more. I shut Tony out as I threw myself into domestic chores and bringing up the children. Tony often spoke to his friends in Greek so that I could not understand. And his mobile would ring at odd times. He would go outside to speak to the caller, then come in and say ruefully: 'I've got to go to Hillingdon. The entry phone's been vandalised again.'

As with the money situation, if I ever questioned his whereabouts or actions he would get defensive and aggressive. I tried to modify my own behaviour to calm him down. I believed him when he blamed me for provoking him. I had this rosy idea that, somehow, if I behaved in a certain way myself, I could influence everyone around me and achieve happy families.

Tony had a quick temper and his verbal tirades left dents in my confidence like bruises on my skin. The tirades eventually led to occasional slaps and meals spattering walls. The first time it happened I felt foolish at my unawareness of the boundaries of his tolerance. I believed that I should have seen it coming, and certainly would in future. Then it became an embarrassing secret. Keeping it quiet was a better alternative to exposing my own frailties in accepting such behaviour.

Tentatively, I started confiding in people that I was unhappy with Tony. But, typically, something good would happen (a pleasant evening with friends, Tony's optimistic proclamations about the future), and I would kid myself that most marriages have difficult times and that we would get through them. Tony reaped my smiles and was able to dissociate completely from his behaviour. I found myself owning it almost as completely as my own behaviour. I hoarded thoughts of our good times in order to bury my head in the sand about the bad. It was obviously an unconscious coping mechanism that echoed the way I reacted when Chrissy had good periods.

Of course, my family became aware of what was going on. I left once with the children to spend a fortnight in a women's refuge. Tony was so tearful and contrite that even my level-headed sister persuaded me I should give him another chance. I went back, but I felt as though I had all the cares in the world on my shoulders. Tony was eight-and-a-half years older than me, yet I felt ancient compared to him.

'It's like being married to a fifty-year-old,' he said.

And, to be honest, I often felt like I had four children, not three!

Though I managed to maintain the children's daily routine and the children got cuddles and affection from us both, their behaviour must have been affected by the marital discord even though they did not witness any violence. It was difficult to tell how aware Chrissy was of tension around her. She did not react straight away if someone else was creating havoc.

I can understand why the pressure of having a learning disabled child breaks couples up, but that was not so in our case. We had our own differences and problems that we tried harder to resolve *because* we had a learning disabled child.

It seemed easier to stay than to leave. I had dug a deep hole for myself having three children with Tony, following blindly the life path that I had mapped out for myself. I was terrified of coping alone with the children. To have money worries, inadequate housing and no support with a child like Chrissy is a daunting prospect. Every time I went along with another unacceptable situation I lost more control over my life and became, as a consequence, more helpless – a recipe for disaster.

CHAPTER 4

Making Contacts

During my third pregnancy Chrissy continued to have regular outbursts. In them, as usual, the intensity never wavered. She had progressed to more elaborate self-harm. She still banged her head, but she also bit her fingers, tried to throw herself downstairs and clawed at her eyes. Her face was often covered in self-inflicted scratches.

When I saw an ad in the paper placed by Contact '81, a local parents' support group for parents of disabled children, I immediately rang the phone number. The lady who answered had three children, two of them twins with tuberous sclerosis – a rare congenital condition associated with epilepsy, skin lesions, lack of muscle power and learning disabilities. I went round to see her and met the rest of the group. We met up monthly in someone's home and discussed our lives.

It was not all doom and gloom. We had a good laugh too. I remember one parent's story about a big, strong teenager with Down's syndrome, who tied his helpless mum to a lamppost outside their local shops. No one batted an eyelid at any of Chrissy's exploits. They had all been there. The children varied in the extent and nature of their disabilities, but being part of this group made me feel less alone. With Contact '81 we went on trips with the children and at Christmas the mums went out on their own for a meal.

I learned more from the group than I had from anyone else. They told me about the orange disabled badges and disability benefits, like invalid care, attendance and mobility allowances. (Attendance and

mobility are combined now and called 'disability living allowance'.)
Most of the parents had older children, and they all said that the
older the child gets the harder you have to fight for everything you
need. Advocating for any child is hard work, but with learning
disabled children it is a lifetime's work.

Some parents throw themselves into all processes stemming from
having a learning disabled child, with amazing energy and drive.
Others drag their feet and remain in denial, shocked at finding
themselves in a world that they never dreamed they would be part of.
Parent groups can help those who have difficulty starting by offering
support. I believe that parents make a mistake not accessing support
groups like this because it validates their isolation and their feelings
of being the only parent with a struggling child. Nevertheless, we
failed to attract more parents of young children into the group as our
children got older. Perhaps they preferred not to know what the
future might hold. There is never a time that reality smacks you
harder in the face than when you see older children with learning
disabilities while yours is still a baby.

By now I had gained more knowledge about the causes of
learning disabilities and had considered the possibility of Chrissy
having a genetic condition. In May 1987 Tony's brother Peter and
his wife Lynda had a third son, Nicholas, who was born with Down's
syndrome. Nicholas was adorable, and his parents came to terms with
his disability only to tragically lose him nearly two years later from
myeloid leukaemia.

A visit to the genetics clinic at Great Ormond Street Hospital
during my third pregnancy reassured us that it was just bad luck, one
family having two disabled children out of nine grandchildren. There
was no connection between Nicholas's disability and Chrissy's. The
geneticists remarked on Chrissy's joint laxity and short stature. They
felt her 'triangular' face was similar to those seen in children with
Russell–Silver syndrome, but this was later excluded by a skeletal
survey. Fragile X, Angelmann syndrome and the unusually named 3M
syndrome were also discounted. The geneticists concluded that they
could not detect a recognisable syndrome in Chrissy and that the

recurrence risks were 3 per cent, not much higher than those of the general population.

Meanwhile our local paediatrician referred Chrissy to Great Ormond Street for investigations into her growth and developmental delay. They said that she was globally retarded, and her maturational 'bone age' (calculated by hand and wrist X-rays) was half her chronological age.

'She'll be late with puberty and is unlikely to grow taller than five feet,' the growth specialist predicted.

Chrissy's height and weight usually remained within the bottom centile of growth charts so there was never a question of doing anything about it with growth hormones.

Chrissy went on a new anticonvulsant medication, Tegretol. She had been off medication for a while but the fits were too frequent to leave it like that. Tegretol had a strange effect on her, making her hyperactive and increasing the amount of fits, though she was on it for a year before we realised that medication could be causing these symptoms. We had already noticed that certain premeds had adverse effects on Chrissy. Also, each time she came round from some general anaesthetics I would have to restrain her because she would go crazy, banging her head on the floor and screaming. The nursing staff were mystified and tended to leave us to our own devices. I felt terribly isolated at times like that, as though I were the only parent in the world whose child reacted this way.

These effects are relatively common amongst people with challenging behaviour and learning disabilities, yet the fact went unacknowledged by any of the medical professionals we came across. We had never been able to give Chrissy Valium for fits or to calm her down in outbursts because it intensified her agitation and prolonged epileptic fits. This is why she often had to be admitted to hospital and given a paraldehyde injection. It was only when Chrissy was given Valium after going into *status epilepticus* that the effect was recorded on the cover of her medical notes and accepted by *all* medical professionals involved in her care. (*Status epilepticus* is a term used whenever one seizure runs into another without the person regaining normal conciousness between seizures.) This incident was likely to have been brought on by the withdrawal of the Tegretol, even though the withdrawal had been gradual to coincide with the introduction of Epilim.

Before going into *status* Chrissy had three major fits then did not come out of a fourth one. Luckily by then we had got her to hospital. The fourth fit was not completely generalised so, although her breathing was laboured, she still took in some oxygen. However, I was terrified permanent harm would come to her as a result of this fit. Despite my assertions about Valium, it was given to Chrissy; and pandemonium broke out as her convulsions increased dramatically and the fit activity intensified. I sat outside the children's ward, leaving her surrounded by medical staff, scared witless, wondering if it would ever end.

Thankfully the fit subsided soon after paraldehyde was given. In all it lasted 45 minutes. If medical staff had taken note of my observations about Chrissy and Valium it would have been a lot shorter. It was frustrating that her reaction to Valium had to take such a dramatic manifestation before doctors would accept my assertions about its effects. Chrissy's reactions to drugs and general anaesthetics showed also that there was more than one cause for her outbursts. They were not just a behavioural reaction to a stressful situation. You could never take anything for granted with Chrissy because she was so unpredictable, both physiologically and behaviourally.

I have rarely heard strangers remark on Chrissy's behaviour. No one has ever suggested (within my earshot anyway) that Chrissy needs a good smack. However, someone who should have known better, another mum of two learning disabled children, displayed her ignorance about challenging behaviour. I had just learnt that we were eligible for an orange disabled badge. Other children we knew had behaviour that made them difficult to manage when out, but they were not all considered severe enough to warrant the badge.

This mum asked me, 'You jammy so-and-so. How come you managed to wangle a badge? I couldn't get one.'

Taken aback, I replied, 'Chrissy's got epilepsy and physical incoordination, but the main reason I got it was because of her behaviour problems.'

'Well, I won't *let* my children have behaviour problems,' she said, curtly.

I was left open-mouthed. How can another parent, most of all one who has children with a recognised syndrome, say something like that? All our children were so different. At times like that I desperately wanted a label to pin on Chrissy so I could say: 'Well, children with this condition often display difficult behaviour.'

A male friend of the family, observing Chrissy when she was five, also aired his views: 'I'd be scared to turn my back on her once she got older in case she stabbed me.'

I think he was confused about the distinction between mental handicap and mental health. Yet even considering that, he was implying that everyone with mental health problems is a potential psychotic killer.

More recently, a friend revealed her prejudices when our mutual friend, Olwen, was discussing the organisation of a meal out for her birthday. Olwen told me that our friend was not able to get a babysitter, and therefore would not be coming. She added: 'I said that you were bringing Chrissy to my house, and had arranged a babysitter there for her. Then I told her that she could use this babysitter for her girls as well.'

'Oh no, I couldn't expose my girls to someone with a handicap. They'd be frightened,' our friend claimed.

'But that's ignorance,' Olwen exclaimed in our defence.

'I can't help the way I feel,' our friend said.

Dealing with such flagrant ignorance is not my main concern, but it hurts.

Chrissy's challenging behaviour only drew the attention of strangers as she grew. When she was little I could pick her up and remove her from situations. Most people do not turn a hair at toddler tantrums. When Chrissy grew too big to carry and I ended up stuck in awkward situations (I have lost count of how many times that has happened) people either averted their eyes or openly gawped. Usually, though, I am too engrossed in trying to deal with the situation to observe what is going on around me.

On some occasions kind strangers have been sympathetic and asked what they could do to help. When Chrissy was about eight she went into an outburst while we were in a shop. My car was about half a mile away up the other end of town and I had the other children with me and bags of shopping. While I was asking a member of staff if I could move Chrissy somewhere until the storm was over, a wonderful stranger offered to help. He carried Chrissy right through the shopping centre to my car, which was in one of the few disabled bays in Hemel Hempstead.

On another occasion I took Chrissy on holiday to Spain with a friend and her toddler. The outward plane journey was an ordeal, with Chrissy screaming the whole way. A kind passenger offered to hold Chrissy while I ate my lunch. I gratefully accepted, and was mortified when Chrissy threw up in her lap! I will never forget the sight of this lady waiting by the luggage carousel with vomit stains all over her dress. Chrissy was unable to locate or communicate pain and I had not realised at the time that in the pressurised cabin she was probably in agony from her blocked-up ears.

Last year I was inundated with offers of help in my local supermarket when Chrissy lay on the floor, screaming. Sometimes distracting Chrissy by giving her a shopping list helps, but not this time. Another shopper who offered help had enough on her plate with two toddlers of her own, so I asked her to locate a burly security guard to help me. Chrissy became well known in this store for her tantrums. She would walk in there calmly, then an unknown trigger would set her off. Maybe it was the hustle and bustle in such a large place. Some artificial lighting seemed to first transfix her then distress her too.

It would be easy to become neurotic about potential triggers for Chrissy's anxiety and distress, but I had to consider every possibility. The film *There's Something about Mary* portrayed an amiable adolescent with learning disabilities who went crazy if anyone touched his ears. If only it were that simple! If Chrissy just had specific fears and phobias we could, at least, try to avoid them.

CHAPTER 5

Beginnings and Endings

Undeterred by my previous holiday experience, I took the plunge again in the summer of 1988 by going to Cyprus with Chrissy, Tony and Jamie. Chrissy had grommets in then but she was still very distressed by the flight. She got a nasty ear infection out there and ended up in hospital because she had febrile fits and an uncontrollably high temperature. The hospital in Limassol, where we had been staying, was basic to say the least. It was lucky that the hospital (being basic) was the sort to have old-fashioned drugs like paraldenhyde. Nursing staff told us that other children were not allowed into the hospital, so one of us had to stay in the apartment while the other one visited Chrissy. We got her out of there as fast as we could.

I had never felt particularly tired during my previous pregnancies but in my third I felt overwhelmed with exhaustion – the kind that makes you feel drugged. Chrissy's medical problems were not the only difficulties I encountered on holiday. We foolishly allowed Jamie to quench his thirst with lots of cola drinks and he became overwhelmingly hyperactive and unmanageable. He craved the fizzy drink and, when he had not had it for a while, shook from head to foot and sobbed bitterly for it – caffeine withdrawal! I avoided cola drinks like the plague for both children after that. When we came back from Cyprus I read something about some children's behaviour and epilepsy being helped by dietary intervention. I wrote to Chrissy's neurologist at Great Ormond Street, mentioning the possibility of her behaviour problems being exacerbated by food intolerances.

However, any thoughts of dietary intervention were put on hold as I neared my due date. I held a chaotic third birthday party at home for Jamie in December 1988. I made him a 'Thomas the Tank Engine' birthday cake and the face kept sliding off! Chrissy had a marvellous time dancing to her favourite record, Queen's *It's a Kind of Magic*. And she loved the birthday food. She prefers picking at buffet food to sitting down for a proper meal.

A week later, on 13 December 1988, our little girl Alex was born at St Albans City Hospital (Hemel Hempstead maternity unit was closed at the time). Her spine was facing mine (posterior presentation) and contractions lasted over 48 hours as she slowly turned around ready for the birth. Nevertheless, because the increase in pain was gradual I managed to have an active, completely drug-free (though by no means painless!) labour. Alex was an easy baby who did everything by the book. Maybe I was not such a bad mum after all. Psychologists might say that I was more relaxed with my third, but things at home were anything but relaxed.

Tony and I were at loggerheads and avoided spending time together. He was often out and I had lost interest in his whereabouts. He never helped with the children when he was at home anyway. We spent a disastrous Christmas at mum's. For some reason, Tony loathed Christmas and spent most of this one muttering under his breath about how awful it all was. He walked out on Christmas Day after engineering a row. He often did that if he needed to escape for some reason.

I have a bittersweet memory of that Christmas. Dad and I had never been close; he was a strict father and was not tactile or affectionate. But his senile dementia softened his brittle edges. And, despite his own suffering, he reached out and held me as I wept over the ashes of my dying marriage. Four years later he would die from a chest infection after becoming bedridden through his disease.

After Christmas I decided that I was no longer prepared to live on a knife-edge at the mercy of Tony's moods. Any love I had for him had completely died. I told Tony I was moving into Chrissy's room. Our marriage was over.

Tony realised that we had reached the end of the line and that he had nothing to lose by confessing to his affairs. I was not surprised when he admitted to seeing eighteen-year-old Tracy Clark for the last two years. I had been getting an increasing number of odd phone calls with the caller hanging up, and Tony's nocturnal 'callouts' to the Hillingdon council blocks where he fitted entry phones had reached an all-time peak. Lots of things clicked into place and I knew I had made the right decision to end our marriage. It was only when I saw a solicitor that I realised that somehow Tony had managed to buy a flat in Berkhamsted with Tracy. Our debts were such that repossession was imminent.

Tony moved out and we put our house up for sale. Not having a clue where or when we would be housed left me reeling with panic. I loved my home – the 'Thomas the Tank Engine' mural on Jamie's wall, Alex's dream nursery with its teddy bear and balloon decorations, and my rustic kitchen with all mod cons. The children each had their own rooms, and having a comfortable, spacious, well-organised home helped me to cope with Chrissy's erratic behaviour.

Being organised is a necessity for families with a learning disabled child to function properly. Routine household tasks are hindered by additional specific demands due to the child's special needs. Havoc can ensue if your life around the child is not properly organised. Then there is a higher likelihood of you losing your temper, which leads to feelings of failure and inadequacy. You can end up neglecting siblings and your husband or partner because of the sheer amount of work involved in caring for a child with learning disabilities and challenging behaviour. Tony often complained: 'I'm just the breadwinner here. You never pay me any attention.'

So you try to fit everything in. But if you work at full capacity you become unable to cope with the many unexpected crises parents of children with challenging behaviour face. This then compounds your feelings of ineffectuality.

I operated on full throttle all the time and therefore found it hard to deal with anything unexpected or unplanned. It was not a good time to be trying out a new treatment for Chrissy, but I was excited and optimistic about a letter I received, while still living in

Bovingdon, from Chrissy's neurologist responding to my enquiry about dietary intervention. He advised me not to embark on any dietary treatment at home and said he would ask a colleague with an interest in food allergies to see Chrissy.

Many doctors argue that, with regard to food, 'allergies' is not the right term because they are not allergies in the traditional sense, in that they are rarely revealed by blood tests and are not life-threatening. Some people prefer to use the terms 'sensitivities' and 'intolerances'.

The neurologist's colleague noted the intermittency of Chrissy's worst behaviour problems and felt it was worth trying dietary treatment. I took Chrissy to see him and he decided to supervise her on an elimination diet known as the 'few foods diet'. For three weeks she was only allowed foods least likely to cause sensitivities, such as turkey, lamb, pears, rice, potatoes, and certain fruits and vegetables. The idea of this was to obtain 'baseline' behaviour. Thereafter, one food a week would be systematically reintroduced and any reaction recorded.

On the first day of the few foods diet Chrissy giggled hysterically and spun autistic-like round the room. I was fascinated and could not wait to see what effect food reintroduction would have. Unfortunately, after a seemingly good start, effects became hard to monitor. I believe that this and similar diets are fundamentally flawed. If children have problems with food sensitivities they are likely to have problems with inhalants too. Imagine trying to figure out if a child has reacted to a newly reintroduced food or the smell of petrol you have just put in your car. It becomes very confusing.

The underlying causes of such food and chemical sensitivities are complex. Books have been written and theories put forward about why they are more common nowadays. There is much cynicism amongst conventional doctors about whether they even exist.

Some foods provoke immediate, obvious reactions; other reactions are unclear and take longer to appear. My sister Sarah worked for a local environmental clinic that helped patients alter their lifestyles to reduce unnecessary exposure to chemicals and inhaled particles. They recommend dietary supplements, and a rotation diet to reduce repeated exposure to certain foods. The clinic also gave neutralising vaccines. They claim to have had some success with autism. I was curious about environmental medicine and still believe that many common illnesses have an environmental component, but the NHS rarely provide funding and I felt that it was a long, complicated road to go down.

The foods that people crave are often the ones that cause them problems. Often after Chrissy binged she had a fit. Chrissy rarely ate anything other than wheat and dairy products, but that may have been due to her obsessional nature. Also the bingeing may have been caused by some biochemical changes from the impending fit, rather than the bingeing causing the fit. When Chrissy appeared to have behavioural reactions it was hard to tell whether she was reacting to one of the 'few foods', an inhalant, a new food I'd reintroduced, Jamie or something else happening around her.

Chrissy continued to exhibit 'autistic-like' behaviours during reintroduction (hand-flapping, giggling, going into her own world, humming, rolling back and forth on the floor, stripping off and grabbing her crutch) and had diarrhoea, discharging ears, sore throats, outbursts, and wetting and soiling accidents.

I made mistakes with the diet. It takes time to get used to reading food labels. For instance, 'modified starch' means that either corn or wheat is included. Food manufacturers do not specify which. I kept slipping up by inadvertently including forbidden ingredients. I was suspicious that Tony did not stick to the diet when Chrissy was with him. It was tiresome to keep reiterating to other people the importance of sticking rigidly to the diet. I am sure that more than one well-meaning person slipped Chrissy biscuits or sweets when I was not around. Also Chrissy was still on Epilim and I wondered whether that would mask the diet's effects.

Both the dietician and Chrissy's consultant at Great Ormond Street Hospital were very supportive and mentioned rotation diets. They also said that there are a small number of children who react to so many foods that dietary control is impractical. I got so confused and had so much else on my plate that I gave it up after six months. Thereafter I became even more conscientious about not feeding any of my children junk food. And I remained vigilant about dramatic mood changes or physical effects after they had eaten certain foods or had been exposed to strong smells.

By June 1989 a psychiatric social worker was visiting me weekly. I needed to sort my life out after the break-up with Tony. And we were having ongoing battles over the divorce settlement.

Jamie started the same pre-school nursery in Bovingdon that Chrissy had attended. Staff said that it was like having Chrissy back and were not sure whether Jamie was just settling in or copying Chrissy. It was hard to tell how much of Chrissy's behaviour Jamie copied. A few times I had found him lying on the floor, dribbling like Chrissy does in a fit. Jamie and Chrissy both wet and soiled themselves after they were out of nappies. My carpets were full of soggy patches where I had cleaned up messes; and my washing machine was always on, filled with bedding and clothes.

Chrissy had started a local school for children with moderate learning difficulties. The staff were reassuring about what they could do for Chrissy. However, getting Chrissy up, breakfasted, dressed and out of the door was a monumental task, especially with two other young children. I organised myself the night before, laying out clothes and putting out breakfast things. But we still had frazzled mornings.

A godsend was that transport to and from Chrissy's school, which was about three miles away, would be provided. But it was not always straightforward. One day her taxi driver knocked on my door.

'She's refusing to wear a seat belt, and I'm not paying the £50 fine,' he snapped.

On other occasions Chrissy wet on car seats, opened windows, threw her shoes, and generally distracted the driver. The drivers would get stroppy with me and impatient with Chrissy. They were not all geared up to learning disabled children. Eventually an escort was provided. It made all the difference.

One morning I had a visit from the police.

'A domestic dispute has been reported at this address,' they said.

'There hasn't been one,' I insisted, puzzled. 'You've made a mistake.'

Unusually, the police told me the name and address of the woman who had reported the dispute. Mystified, I looked her phone number up and rang her. She said that she walked her dog past my house every morning and had heard children screaming. That morning she had heard me shouting too, and wondered if the children were being hurt.

When I found out what time she had walked past it clicked into place. That was when I usually did Chrissy's hair in her bedroom at the front of the house. She always screamed the place down because she loathed her head being touched. This morning I had yelled back at her.

'Today was mild by normal standards,' I laughed.

I explained the situation but she remained unconvinced. I even asked her round for a cup of tea so she could see for herself that the children were unharmed. She turned my offer down. It is a good job she did not come round that evening. I cut Chrissy's fringe and she went bananas!

Chrissy's tantrums were becoming more destructive. She threw things, stripped her clothes off and hurt herself in every way imaginable. She became obsessed with buttons and switches and stuck things in electric sockets. The school was also finding Chrissy's behaviour a problem. It was disruptive to the other children and prevented her from learning.

Because of the Jekyll and Hyde nature of some of her challenging behaviour I still had good days with Chrissy. I spent a day once with some mums whose children went to the same school as Chrissy, and she behaved impeccably. I felt so proud of her. Afterwards we went to see dad, who was in a nursing home by now. His condition was deteriorating rapidly. The children were fine there and dad seemed pleased to see them in moments of lucidity. Jamie was not sure about the 'hollible ladies' there who wailed and mumbled as they sat blank-eyed and insubstantial in their chairs.

During the summer of 1990 I felt like I was living on borrowed time, stuck behind a brave face while things were crumbling around me. I would cook Sunday dinner for friends in exchange for their help with the children. I felt panicky at the thought of being alone with

Chrissy and her outbursts. It had been my decision to separate, and I had no regrets about ending my marriage, but the implications of being alone with three children, especially one with a severe disability, suddenly hit me with the force of a juggernaut.

CHAPTER 6

Struggling Alone

Because of Chrissy's learning disabilities I had to disperse the children if I wanted to go out because no one would have all three. Tony and his girlfriend, Tracy, sometimes had one or two of the children, and my sister and mum occasionally had the other, or others. Sometimes they would have the children just so that I could catch up on my sleep.

Chrissy went through a phase of trying every trick in the book to avoid going to bed. She made herself vomit and deliberately soiled and wet herself. Tony and I had made the mistake of having her in with us so that we could get some sleep. I had been too exhausted to deal with it. You need to sort that habit out from a position of strength because it gets worse before it gets better. It was something I was determined to clamp down upon now I was on my own.

Chrissy's fit pattern changed in that they occurred mainly at night. She also went through cycles of bizarre night-time outbursts where she would try to climb into drawers and appeared to halluc- inate. Jamie was a 5am riser and Alex, despite being content during the day, was wakeful at night. So between them they ensured I hardly had any sleep.

Other times when I had childcare I went out with friends. Female friends were very important to me during that time. I was still under thirty and had both single and married friends. If I could not get sitters, just having friends round for a game of Trivial Pursuit or Pictionary was therapy. Maybe I was constantly on the verge of hysteria, but I have never laughed so much as I did during that period

– real side-splitting belly laughs over the most ridiculous things. I found that I was able to drink alcohol again. Since my pregnancies I used to slide down walls after one glass of wine! I did not drink alone but I used alcohol as a temporary release when in the company of friends. After a time I realised the depressive effect alcohol has on you the next day. Waking up to reality every morning was bad enough without a hangover!

It is important to have a good support system through family and friends as well as professionals. The first time support services offered respite was in 1989 in the form of a temporary befriender. We never got our own permanent one, maybe because of Chrissy's challenging behaviour. Our befriender looked after Chrissy in her own home. Chrissy stayed with her on the day of my nephew Nicholas's funeral, and she had Chrissy overnight when I became ill the following year. Her help at those times was invaluable. It is essential not to feel guilty about needing a break from your child. Having a break relaxes and rejuvenates you, therefore making you a better parent for your child.

We were living on income support, and the negative equity on the house was mounting up as the DSS only pays interest on the mortgage. (Getting that paid was yet another battle.) Tony appeared to be unable to support us because of his own financial difficulties. If the house was not sold by the end of the year it would be repossessed by our mortgage provider. They were likely to reduce the price for a quick sale, therefore leaving us with higher debts. I faced losing my car as well as my home. The finance company that we had used to buy my Volvo was on my back.

I had no way of telling how all these stresses affected Chrissy. There were still no obvious triggers to her mood changes much of the time and I noticed no deterioration in her behaviour. Fortunately Alex was too young to realise what was going on. However, Jamie was a different story. He was distraught every time his dad dropped him home after a stay. Sometimes Tony took him back with him because Jamie did not want him to leave, or he rang to say that Jamie was upset at the thought of coming home. Could he stay another night? It is natural for children to show distress at the thought of separation from a parent, even if just for a short time. Jamie did not cry for long once his dad dropped him home but his general behaviour deteriorated. Tony badgered me to let Jamie live with him and Tracy and even threatened to take him to live in Cyprus.

Tony's behaviour prior to the financial settlement over our divorce was erratic to say the least. One minute he was begging me to try again; the next he was making threats about money and Jamie. I felt intimidated and confused, and started to wonder if everything I did was destined to go wrong. Was there something I did that brought out the worst in others?

At the end of 1989 sadness was a live thing with claws always lurking behind my back. I looked at the world through grey-tinted glasses. I did not want to spend the next decade or so as a single mum reliant on income support, yet I did not imagine that I would be in a position to get a job for some time. I had trained as a secretary and the only way I could work would be during school hours. A part-time job would not pay enough to support us, and Alex had a few years to go before starting full-time school. If I eventually managed to get full-time work how would I get childcare for Chrissy?

I was lonely and still young, but the prospect of meeting someone else was bleak too. Anyone contemplating a serious relationship with me would have to be prepared to put up with Chrissy and her problems. If I remarried or a boyfriend moved in I would lose my income support, and he would feel forced into supporting us financially. Tony was on family credit and only paid me the minimum £15 per child.

I had regular visits from the psychiatric social worker. He did not offer solutions at first. But he tried to help me to make sense of what was happening in the exhausting chaos of my life. I needed to unload to someone about my feelings as well as talk about the children's problems.

Interactions between the two older children were still negative much of the time, if they occurred at all. Generally they played separately. Chrissy preferred adult attention to mixing with other children. She often followed me around using repetitive, meaningless phrases and demanding responses. If I ignored her, she worked herself up into a frenzy and became very anxious, often leading to a full-blown outburst. Yet if I answered her, the same question or phrase would still be repeated endlessly throughout the day. Left to her own devices she was purposelessly destructive at times, ripping books and pulling toys apart. The jigsaw puzzles and drawing that she used to enjoy only held her attention for very short periods. I had to instigate and supervise play. At school they were finding her increasingly demanding too.

I received a letter from her teacher stating that Chrissy had bitten a little boy on the cheek. I asked if they had any suggestions about how I could stop her biting (she did it at home too). They said that they had none but that they could not allow it to happen again. What did they intend to do if it did? They said that they would arrange for us to see a child psychiatrist.

Having a disabled sibling forced Jamie, and later Alex, to grow up far too quickly. On one occasion Alex fell down the stairs when I left her with Jamie in his bedroom, foolishly expecting him to keep an eye on her while I dealt with one of Chrissy's outbursts. Poor Alex got the thin end of the wedge as far as being physically hurt went. Chrissy could inadvertently kick out at her in a tantrum. Alex could not always move fast enough to get out of the way. Sometimes Chrissy would deliberately poke or hit her just for the hell of it. Jamie, quite understandably, was extremely jealous of Alex and tended to be rough with her at times. This jealousy is common in toddlers feeling usurped by a younger sibling. Jamie's needs had already been subordinated by having a disabled sibling, so maybe his reactions were more exaggerated than usual. The first night at home after Alex's birth he heard her crying in her cot and muttered: 'Take that *thing* back to the hostible.'

I am gratified that Alex has appeared to be unaffected by the furore going on around her during those early years.

A note I made in my diary one gloomy November day when Chrissy was still only five, Jamie nearly four and Alex 11 months gives an insight into a typical day then. It read:

> Woke up with yet another heavy cold (I had colds more often than I was well!). Chrissy had an outburst, and accidentally

slammed the door on Jamie's fingers. He was too inconsolable to go to play-school, then he 'stabbed' her above the eye with a plastic toy. This all happened before 9am! To cap it all Alex was ill with diarrhoea. (She had been under the weather like this for weeks and it turned out to be rotavirus, a major cause of gastroenteritis.)

The bad times were interspersed with occasional brighter times. In November 1989 Jamie's teacher said that he was settling down well and learning to share with other children, though he still had tantrums over trivial things. I received a positive note from Chrissy's teacher. She said that they had experienced a lovely morning with Chrissy, and she had remembered four pictures on cards after they had been turned over. Her teacher wrote that it showed she had some memory and comprehension skills. It was the first time that I had noted any real progress since Chrissy started there.

Chrissy's behaviour continued to be inconsistent and unpredictable. My stomach was often in knots before she was due home from school. Over the next year I felt pushed into a corner and was to make a momentous decision that would affect our family's lives for ever. I did what I thought best at the time but decisions made in haste are rarely the right ones. I was in no state emotionally to realise the long-term implications.

CHAPTER 7

Sinking into Depression

After getting information from the mums at the support group, I applied for attendance allowance. The doctor who visited me at home sounded confident that I would receive the high rate for day and night-time care. The extra money would help to make life more bearable. The additional costs incurred by having a learning disabled child included those of constantly washing wet bedding and clothes, and replacing household objects, books and toys that Chrissy broke. My carpets needed cleaning regularly because of all the accidents. Kitchen tiles needed replacing and wallpaper was regularly torn and scuffed. Chrissy sometimes ripped her clothes too. There were frequent trips to Great Ormond Street Hospital that I discovered belatedly I could claim travel expenses for whilst on income support. You take these extra costs for granted when you have a child with disabilities and challenging behaviour, but they mount up.

My decree nisi came through in January 1990. That same month I started seeing John, then 28, a single man who still lived with his parents. I was in no fit state emotionally to get involved with any man while my life was in such turmoil, especially one like John. He brought fun and laughter into my life but I soon learned that he was terrified of committing himself to any woman, let alone a soon-to-be divorcee with three children, one moreover with severe learning disabilities. Insultingly, he kept our relationship secret from his family and friends. He also had a massive chip on his shoulder about women who had hurt him in the past. He dumped his emotional baggage on my already bowed shoulders, then justified his behaviour by making remarks like: 'I'm in control of my life now and I like it that way. If I'd met you years ago you'd have only messed me about like all the rest.'

Somehow I found the strength to end contact with him after five roller-coaster months. This latest blow destroyed my last shred of optimism and my health. I had passively allowed another unacceptable situation to happen.

In February I had a period that carried on and on. The bleeding got heavier and showed no signs of abating. When hormone tablets failed to stem the flow my GP had me admitted to West Herts Hospital. Luckily, the temporary befriender was able to look after Chrissy for me. No cause was found for the bleed, and I had several more afterwards with further hospital stays and courses of hormone tablets. This led, seven years later, to a hysterectomy.

The bleeding drained me even more. I lost my appetite and the weight fell off me as I sank into the gloom of black coffee and cigarettes. I developed a nervous tic in one eye (I felt like the character driven mad by Inspector Clouseau in the Pink Panther films!) and I bit my nails to the quick. I became obsessed with certain classical and pop songs and played them over and over again. I had one virus after another and felt constantly exhausted. Mornings were the worst. I was full of dread about what the day ahead held.

One day early in 1990 I wrote in my diary:

> Woke up feeling totally desolate with a big, black pit opening up in front of me. I can't keep body and soul together for much longer. I feel pathetic and weak. God knows what's the matter with me.

I had never suffered mental illness and had no idea that symptoms such as feeling awful in the morning are a sign of clinical depression. I blamed it on my defences being low after sleep. Using sleep to escape from life is another sign; I slept at every opportunity. I could no longer accept all life had to throw at me. I had to get my family out of this mire. The trouble is, I did not know where to start.

Friends and family tried to help but eventually lost patience with me. Like me, they did not realise that I was ill and was no longer able to help myself. It is the typical 'pull yourself together' scenario. Dad was in the nursing home, but mum was still too traumatised by the experience of caring for him and seeing his disease destroy him to give me the support I needed with the children.

I could not take my eyes off any of my children for a moment. One day Chrissy took my lipstick from my bedroom drawer and drew over everything in my room. Jamie pulled a shelf full of toys down on top of himself. Alex had become mobile and was at that exploring stage where nothing is safe. The depression made me feel even more helpless when faced with Chrissy's challenging behaviour. Each time she had an outburst, I felt even more convinced that it was due to something I had done wrong.

And my demanding but loving son became a defiant, aggressive four-year-old. When I sent him to his room he would scream blue murder and bang his beloved toy cars on the door, leaving great dents in it. Some children appear to escape unscathed from divorce. Sensitive children like Jamie suffer long-term effects. But then it has to be remembered that, unlike the others, he was at an age where he was aware of what was going on. He also spent far more time with his dad than either Chrissy or Alex.

I felt that I was losing him and questioned his hostility to me. I was painfully aware that his dad spoke about our conflicts in front of Jamie. If Tony is angry with someone he lets the world know. He also informed me that Jamie called Tracy 'mum'. He still called me 'mummy' too. It haunts me now to think about what Jamie must have gone through during this awful time. An additional factor affecting Jamie was my depression.

Every time I tried to find solutions to certain parts of my predicament I hit brick walls. Hope slowly tipped away until I looked at the future and despaired.

As I wrote in the previous chapter, I struggled to accept that I would be dependent on income support. One solution could be to use my time at home to study for work that I could do around the children. One avenue I pursued was the possibility of a career as a dietician. I enjoyed cooking and was fascinated by the effect of diet on behaviour and health. I wrote off for the relevant information. But in March I received a letter from the Dietetics Association that put paid to any ideas I had in that direction. I would have had to do a four-year full-time course – impossible with Chrissy.

Invalid care allowance is paid to parents who are unable to work because they are caring for their handicapped child. I was eligible for it, but it made no difference to my finances because an equivalent amount was deducted from my income support.

By May 1989 I felt broken and brittle. Everything seemed to be dragging on – the house sale, the divorce, problems with the children. I cannot say if I would have suffered from depression if Chrissy's challenging behaviour was the only factor affecting my life. But it certainly played a major part and made the business of everyday coping more difficult.

Life kept throwing punches at me that I could no longer duck. Each new blow brought me lower until I had no resilience left. I could no longer bear the sight of my own reflection in the mirror. And I only had to see Chrissy flapping her hands and my eyes would well with tears. I broke down in public places too and was brought home more than once by exasperated friends. I could not control when and where I cried. Sometimes I could barely get up because I could not stop crying.

I had unfounded prejudices against antidepressant drugs, believing them to be addictive. I fought my depression. I wanted to slob around all day and not bother getting dressed, but I forced myself to. I knew that if I slipped any further downwards I would go under. Relying on my faith in the resilience of youth, I thought that I could get my act together on my own.

One day in June I lay on my bed to shut out the world. I just could not hold my head together and spiralled downwards into black despair. I felt shaken to my roots and could not stop crying. I phoned mum and she came round with a friend of mine. I was inconsolable and mum did not know what to do with me. She phoned my GP for help, but he did not offer to come round. As mum tried to explain how bad things had got, he kept repeating: 'Talk to her. She needs someone to talk to.' Mum insisted that it had got beyond that but he did not have any other suggestions. I pleaded for someone to get me a bed in a psychiatric unit. I do not know what I hoped to achieve but I was not able to look after myself, let alone the children. I wanted to relinquish my responsibilities until I recovered.

Between mum and a friend temporary childcare was organised. Chrissy's emergency befriender came to the rescue again, by having Chrissy for one night. Tony had Jamie, and mum looked after Alex. My sister came round with some Valium, and my friend took me under her wing. The break from the children was all too short. It was like putting a plaster on a festering wound. When Chrissy came back she had a day of relentless outbursts and misery.

Dread stalked me, then fisted in my belly when Tracy rang to say that she was bringing Jamie back. I did not plan what I said to Tracy. All I knew was that if something did not give *right now* I would snap. I found myself telling Tracy that Tony could have what he had been repeatedly asking for – Jamie. I will never be able to justify caving in, but I had run out of options. Stark reality slapped me: I could not meet all my children's needs. I could not even meet my own. At the time, I could not see the big picture. And I did not foresee the long-term outcome, the emotional problems that Jamie would suffer as a result. How blind I was.

Tony had always urged: 'Jamie would be better off with us. We can offer him a good home. Tracy loves him, and you've got too much on your plate with the three of them. Accept that you can't cope anymore.'

Once I had made my decision, I convinced myself that Jamie *would* be better off there. He enjoyed spending time with his dad and Tracy. Tracy was lovely with the children, and Tony seemed settled and content with her. There were no signs of Tony's mood swings, and I naively put it down to Tracy being more placid and adaptable than me. I was not yet aware enough of destructive behaviour patterns to realise that Tony might behave in the same way with her and Jamie as he had with me.

I have agonised ever since over my decision to let Jamie live with his father. Unsurprisingly, Jamie suffered feelings of rejection and abandonment. And it was hard for him to understand that I love him as much as his sisters. The reason Jamie went to his dad's were practical ones – because he was the least dependent of the three, was about to start full-time school and was the one Tony had asked to have.

Unless you have been there it is hard to appreciate the mixed feelings induced by having to part with a child to survive as a family. The separation is often precipitated by ill health or desperation. In my case it was both. Given that situation again and more knowledge of the services that are available I would have been more forceful earlier on in asking for emergency respite care for Chrissy or approaching social services for hands-on home support to see us through this appalling time. Sending Chrissy to a residential school was not even an option I considered then. She was still, to all intents and purposes, a baby.

There are so many 'ifs' involved here. My family were only too aware of the state I was in; they still insist I took the only route open to me at that time. My depression had become severe. I can only describe it as feeling like bits of me had fragmented. I was convinced that I would never be 'whole' again. Friends and family ran around like headless chickens trying to help me. Even Tony looked shocked when he saw how thin I was. Eating just made me feel nauseous. Everything else rapidly came to a head.

My car was falling apart. Every other day something else went on it. I desperately needed it but could not afford to keep it on the road for much longer. Potential buyers arrived in their droves to view the house. It was a bargain. My solicitor said that we had to drop the price further to sell it as quickly as possible because repossession was imminent and would only incur higher debts.

On my solicitor's advice I visited my local council's housing department and explained that we would soon be homeless and we were broke. I saw a housing officer there who had not got my notes. He said that he would come and see me at home but could not say when. It left me feeling dreadfully insecure. On friends' advice I rang social services and made an appointment with my doctor to get letters for the housing officer, hoping to convince him of my family's compelling housing needs. What terrified me was the thought of moving into a hostel for the homeless with the children. I had visions of us all sleeping in one room and Chrissy waking everyone up with her screaming.

When I saw another GP for my heavy bleeding she patted my knee comfortingly and I burst into tears. She confirmed that the symptoms I was having were typical of depression, and explained why it occurs.

'Quite honestly, I'd have been surprised if you hadn't become depressed with everything that's happened,' she said. 'You have reactive depression. It's an illness, and you can't just "pull yourself together".'

She prescribed a month's course of antidepressants and said that they would take effect in about a week. She allayed my fears about addiction and side-effects, and explained how they worked. Before I left the surgery she said that I could ring any of the doctors at any time if I needed to. Her words helped me a great deal. Knowing that I was ill made me feel less ashamed about falling apart.

The day I started taking the antidepressants I was still having crazy moments when I felt like driving my car into a brick wall. Then in the evening I looked at the children and thought: 'They've got to be my purpose in life.' Though in all honesty I did not genuinely feel I had a purpose.

A week later I still cried on and off all day. I could not be on my own, yet I could not be with people. I could not settle to anything. I stayed at mum's and slept and slept. Sleep was not the escape it had been. I was having unpleasant dreams and waking up feeling even more desolate. I was caught up in this strange nightmare world of my own mind. I rang the doctor and she recommended I double the dose. She told me to come back in another week if that did not work, when she would give me a stronger antidepressant.

The psychiatric social worker gave me food for thought the next day when we discussed entrenched patterns that people repeat in life without realising. I could not change what had happened. But I could change within it. He asked me if I knew that depression was anger turned inwards.

I replied: 'No, I didn't. But, I *am* angry, angry with myself for letting things happen to get us into this state.'

Part 2

Coming Through

Help and Recognition of Difficulties

CHAPTER 8

More Support

So many events occurred together over August and September 1990, when Chrissy was six, that I could not pin my recovery on any single one. It was probably a combination of everything.

I had one less child to deal with after Jamie went to live with his dad. The housing officer came to see me at home and was far more 'human'. I felt hopeful about avoiding a temporary stay in a hostel.

Despite my failure with the dietary treatment, our consultant at Great Ormond Street Hospital gave me further support by writing a letter to the Family Fund Trust, which provides financial help for families looking after very disabled children under 16. The Family Fund Trust quickly responded to the consultant's letter and sent me a cheque to cover the cost of a week-long caravan holiday in Yarmouth. Chrissy had been accepted for a MENCAP-run holiday, and the idea was for me to go when she was away in August. A friend and I took Alex with us. The break was just what I needed, and I came back refreshed with enough energy to deal with my housing situation.

The antidepressants started kicking in. It was like a slow awakening. I became interested in life again and did not dread getting up in the mornings. I joined a pub quiz team, told dirty jokes, played with the children, practised the piano, experimented with recipes and did cryptic crosswords with mum.

I started thinking about the possibility of emerging from all this a stronger person, rather than the diminished person I thought I would be. I was in no doubt that the depression *had* changed me forever, but maybe it was no bad thing. I had no problems weaning myself off my antidepressants. I would not hesitate to take them again if, God forbid, I ever suffer from clinical depression again. I had bad days and more tears but gradually the good days overtook the bad ones.

Just before my thirtieth birthday I met Ian Alcock, then 28. He lived in a rented house in Kings Langley in Hertfordshire, a long way from his family home in Newcastle-under-Lyme. He worked in Beaconsfield as a project engineer and did not seem fazed when I told him about my children. I pulled no punches in describing life with Chrissy. What struck me was Ian's interest in all aspects of my life, including the children. He was quiet, steady, intelligent and good-looking. I was wary and wanted to take things slowly. He understood and let me set the pace.

In October 1990, two weeks before the sale of my house was due to go through, Ian and some friends helped me move into a three-bedroom end of terrace home in Hemel Hempstead. It had no carpets and needed decorating, so I had my work cut out organising it all. The council either decorate it for you (but you cannot choose how) or they offer you redemption vouchers to exchange for decorating materials. I chose redemption vouchers.

Ian met the whole family for dinner at mum's. He accepted the children unreservedly and thought they were sweet and funny. Chrissy was on form. She kept nagging her Uncle Anthony about what was for dinner. 'I don't know – you tell me,' he eventually snapped back.

'Roast beef!' she screamed at him.

It became a standing joke after that. I took Chrissy and Alex for haircuts after Chrissy had finished school one day. Chrissy lay on the floor shouting 'Roast beef!' at the top of her voice. Then she embarrassed me by asking loudly, 'Have you done a poo?'

Being out in public with Chrissy was either an ordeal or a laugh a minute. If I was on my own when Chrissy kicked off, or said and did something inappropriate, I would ignore everyone and grimly deal with it. Afterwards I would have the post-mortem and sometimes see the funny side. Having another adult with me made all the difference. It made Chrissy easier to cart off, if necessary, and helped to defuse potentially explosive situations with humour.

Car journeys were difficult. Ian's parents lived in Newcastle-under-Lyme, about three hours' drive away in Staffordshire. We started visiting for weekends. Luckily his family welcomed my children. Ian's mum, Floss, used to work at a special school and had endless patience with Chrissy. Routine outings were still nerve-racking. Even a trip into the town centre to buy school shoes or to get Chrissy a haircut was a trial. She was far more difficult to manage away from home than at home. So many factors contribute to this. And the more triggers parents and carers can identify, the better they are equipped to deal with the child's challenging behaviour. Known triggers for Chrissy are crowds and large, noisy places. Also, she hates the feel of wind and rain on her skin.

Changing from one activity or environment to another – 'beginnings' and 'ends' – is difficult for her. Even minor changes like going in and out of shops and getting in and out of the car can trigger major tantrums. Chrissy also gets upset when her clothing is not just right: the seams of her socks need to be lined up properly, and she has to have her cuffs turned up and buttons done up. Queueing, eating, and calling round to see someone who has gone out are all very difficult for Chrissy to handle. The worst outbursts coincided with changes of environment such as coming in from school. It did not help that she was tired then too.

For some outbursts, there were obvious triggers, like change or tiredness. Others seemed inherently part of her, and we could not pinpoint any trigger. She could be playing quite happily, doing something I know she enjoys. Then she'd go into 'yes/no' cycles where she'd obsess about something, say cheese on toast. I'd make it for her, then she'd throw it or refuse it, yet still obsess about it. I'd try to reason with her, saying: 'Look, you've got cheese on toast.' But she would seemingly not process that information because she'd still scream: 'I want cheese on toast.'

Sometimes she would move on to another obsession, some compulsion that I couldn't meet or she wouldn't accept. In these states she would get increasingly out of control. Ignoring her wasn't effective.

Distraction only worked if you intervened early, and then it was only intermittently effective. But sometimes there appeared to be no warning signs, just an immediate, intense explosion. I recognised times when Chrissy was so out of her depth that all I could do was wait it out and minimise any damage she did to herself, others or property. Though if we were out it was impractical to sit for over an hour with a screaming, self-abusive child. As Chrissy grew it became more and more difficult to go anywhere. Even going up the road for a pint of milk was a potential minefield. I often came home shattered after being stuck in a public place with Chrissy screaming and refusing to get up (she had become quite a weight by then). It brought those familiar helpless feelings to the fore again.

My health had improved since the depression ended but it was still poor, probably owing to the ongoing stress. I caught every bug going, and developed irritable bowel syndrome and psoriasis. I have a curved spine and my back is structurally weak anyway; I suffered intermittent sciatica and the extra strain caused by lifting Chrissy took its toll. I tried to eat healthily and took supplements to boost my immune system. I frequently struggled with and lost my battle to give up smoking. I blamed it on school holidays because it was invariably at those times that I took up the habit again.

I started exercising regularly to keep the muscles around my spine strong. I went with friends to council-run 'Women for Leisure' sessions at a community centre. We were able to use the creche for our children. I tried Chrissy there once when she was off school, but she upset all the babies and toddlers with her screaming and throwing toys. Halfway through the session one of the helpers approached me and asked me to take her home.

'She's a health and safety risk,' she explained apologetically.

I could hear uproar in the creche as she spoke. All heads swivelled in my direction, and I left feeling embarrassed and furious with Chrissy, then upset with myself for feeling so angry.

I used home videos as well as going to classes. The keep-fit video became one of Chrissy's favourites; it was hilarious watching her do workouts using baked bean cans as weights.

Support services started moving. The psychiatric social worker had suggested on a previous visit that it was time to look at respite care for Chrissy. The local community mental handicap team contacted me and offered help in the form of respite and a clinical psychologist for Chrissy. I went to visit a respite home in Harpenden and found it pleasant, and the staff caring and warm. I spent time with Chrissy on her first afternoon there. She loved it and screamed all the way home because she wanted to stay! She later moved more locally, and we were allocated a certain number of nights in the year. A form was sent out regularly for us to fill in our preferred dates; respite services would fulfil our preferences as best they could.

Respite care helped to break up school holidays and gave us the odd weekend day off. The break is not just for parents, it is for the disabled child and siblings too. At respite there was adequate support for Chrissy to go on outings and she could spend time with her peers. We could go on family outings without having the day spoilt, or just relax at home. I was more able to deal with Chrissy, and Alex was more patient with her after a break.

Around this time, the clinical psychologist paid me a visit and gave me forms to fill in to see if there was any pattern to Chrissy's behaviour. She then came up with suggestions on how to improve some aspects of it. (More on behaviour programmes later.) I visited our local paediatrician and told him that Chrissy had been fit-free for a few months. We decided to wean her off her medication, Epilim, to see what would happen. She had been 'bingey' on it and had gained too much weight. I dressed her in maternity-style loose tops and elasticated trousers because her belly was enormous. (I was amused when one doctor described it as 'trunkal obesity'!)

I discovered at a routine hearing check in October 1992 that Chrissy was deaf in her left ear. It had nothing to do with glue ear or scar tissue from repeated perforations of the eardrum; it was due to nerve deafness. The specialist said that he did not think a hearing aid would benefit her, and would probably even distress her. Glasses to help her long-vision and alternating squint never lasted very long before getting thrown or crushed.

Specialist services became necessary in every aspect of Chrissy's life. I took Chrissy to the dentist for a routine check-up and, despite the dentist giving her latex gloves to play with (Chrissy has a thing about gloves, especially latex ones!), she panicked and bit him. Alex, after seeing Chrissy's distress, also refused to let the dentist examine her. Chrissy was referred to Bushey Dental Hospital, which treats people with learning disabilities. The plan was to bring her for regular visits until she got used to the place, then gradually to encourage her to yield to an examination. But Chrissy seemed to forget what happened previously between each visit. Health professionals try to reason gently with her when they need to examine her, but it can make her more uneasy. They were better off rolling their sleeves up and getting on with it. As she grew older she became more amenable to gentle persuasion because her comprehension skills got a little better. Because Chrissy's vocabulary was wide and she was able to assess situations and use learnt phrases appropriately, people expected more of her than she was capable of, but her comprehension skills were still way behind.

Chrissy sometimes co-operated up to a point with dental examinations, but any treatment necessitated a general anaesthetic. Chrissy eventually had fillings and a special coating put on her teeth under anaesthetic to protect them from decay. She was at risk because she did not chew or clean her teeth thoroughly, though I cleaned her teeth myself as best I could. Her gums were hypertrophic (abnormally enlarged), probably as a result of early use of phenytoin, an anticonvulsant. Thankfully, she did not have the screaming habdabs after this particular anaesthetic. There may be another explanation for this: perhaps she had woken in pain after previous anaesthetics; this dental treatment would not have hurt her.

At the end of February 1991 events overtook me again when two social security officials arrived and quizzed me about Ian staying with us. Someone had phoned the DSS anonymously. It was a nasty feeling, knowing that I had an unseen enemy.

It was like Big Brother. They knew everything about my life and Ian's. Ian was still living at his house in Kings Langley, and paying rent there. I enjoyed cooking him meals and sometimes he would stay over. We were building on our deepening relationship. Luckily, I was able to prove that Ian still lived at his own house. There was nothing of his around the house, and the officials left satisfied that there was no basis to the anonymous allegations. However, this meant we had to make a decision about me staying on or coming off income support. Staying overnight was putting my income support at risk – Ian had to either move in or stop staying over. I rang Ian at work and, without hesitation, he said he would move in. Our relationship was already going in that direction, but I felt pushed into a corner. However, things worked out well.

The children became attached to Ian and he treats them with firmness, humour and affection. Alex adores him, and the feeling is mutual. Ian has worked at building a relationship with Jamie too. Jamie tries to chip away at Ian's boundaries but he has grown to respect Ian and seek his approval because Ian takes the time to listen to him. People have said to me: 'Isn't Ian marvellous taking on your kids?' He is. There are times when he has felt the strain but he became as committed and devoted to their happiness as I am. We settled into a routine with Jamie visiting regularly and Tony seeing the girls. Tony and I managed to be civil to each other. However, what happened next took us back to square one.

Two years after Jamie went to live with Tony and Tracy they split up, which meant further upheaval and loss for Jamie. Tony was in no state to support Jamie through his distress; he was too distraught himself. The full repercussions of Jamie going to live with his dad were becoming apparent. Jamie's behaviour gave me clues that all was not well at home. He would not talk to me about it so I encouraged him to approach his teacher. It resulted in social services becoming involved and removing him from his father pending a child protection investigation.

Jamie came to me for a month. He was either withdrawn or disruptive. To see his sad, bewildered little face was heartbreaking. He was devastated about 'getting his daddy into trouble' and kept asking, tearfully: 'When am I going home?' I fully understood why Jamie wanted to return there. He loved his dad more than anything, and his life was well established there with his school, friends and home life. However, Jamie's behaviour gradually started to settle down while he was with me. I believe that time would have healed much of his anguish about leaving his dad. I tried pleading my case to keep him. But social workers said that he could return to his father's. They never asked me why he went to his father's in the first place. They just took the situation at face value, with the view that Jamie's wishes were paramount. Of course the child's wishes should be taken into account. But what about the child's needs? Children's wishes and needs are not always compatible. Do they know what is best for them at six?

Jamie became even more secretive after he went back to his dad's. He drew a line around what went on there, spiky as barbed wire. It must have taken tremendous courage to speak out to his teacher. And, when he had, it had parted him from the person he loved most. My advice had led to his confiding; therefore, in his eyes, I had betrayed him. I thought I had completely burnt my bridges at that point. The whole business reinforced Jamie's hostility towards me. Fighting a legal battle over Jamie would not have solved anything. It would have pitted Tony against me, causing further split loyalties in Jamie. And without social services' backing I would probably lose, then what further emotional damage would protracted wrangling do to Jamie?

I did not hate Tony. It was all just so terribly sad. Despite all that happened, there is no doubt that Tony loves Jamie. Maybe Tony meets needs in him that I never could. Jamie has always needed lots of attention, and at Tony's he had no siblings to compete with. I understood how the situation had got so out of control. Both Jamie and Chrissy had driven me to the brink with their behavioural outbursts. But you have to get a grip. I resigned myself to hoping that, with support from social services, Jamie and his dad might be able to work through their difficulties. They were meant to be under social services' supervision for a year, but after one visit their social worker left satisfied that everything was OK. However, I remained vigilant about Jamie's welfare, which made him even more reluctant to see me. I had to work doubly hard to regain his trust. It took years.

Jamie's opinion of women must have been very low then because he spoke contemptuously about Tracy, using crude adult language to express his views. He masked his pain with anger, especially towards me. I understood how threatened he felt. But I did not know how to deal with it, especially when his behaviour disturbed Chrissy's equilibrium. Nevertheless, I was determined to maintain regular contact. No matter what distorted view Jamie had of me, I would not let him forget that I was his mother and only wanted the best for him. No matter how badly he behaved I told him that I loved him, and continued to be involved in his life.

I had a complicated juggling act on my hands, trying to meet all my children's needs. Many people who do not know our full story are critical of me over Jamie. I am critical of myself, but I have learned over time that it is unhelpful to keep agonising about it. I need to be strong for Jamie and his siblings. And I am doing my utmost to deal with the situation as it is now.

CHAPTER 9

Outings and Holidays

My divorce was finalised in March 1991. The psychiatric social worker made his last visit then. I felt confident about the future and grateful to him for prompting me to examine the old destructive patterns that had led to my breakdown. I was determined not to repeat them, and the only way to do that was to take more control of my life. As I wrote in the introduction, passive acceptance is the most common but least effective method used by parents to cope with challenging behaviour. I had used it in too many areas of my life.

Chrissy's behaviour off her anticonvulsant drugs had deteriorated. There were less calm periods. She had developed a new and messy form of self-harm – rubbing her nose viciously until it bled. In May her teacher wrote in her home/school book that they had experienced the most difficult day they could remember with her.

Chrissy's fits worsened. Her school reported regular episodes where she would look as though she was about to have a fit, then nothing more would happen. She often looked vague too. The reciprocal relationship between fits and outbursts was not apparent any more. At night Chrissy had screaming episodes again. I wondered if they were a form of night terror. They would occur about two hours after Chrissy had gone to sleep. She would scream as if frightened of something, then immediately go into fifth gear, inconsolable sometimes for two hours. One night she had four of these episodes. It was heartbreaking. As before, there seemed to be nothing I could do to stop them.

I also noticed a new problem. Chrissy developed facial tics. She frequently screwed her eyes up and grimaced. Her face was so lovely when it was relaxed, but she had begun to look more unusual because of these facial expressions and her hand-flapping. Because of a deterioration in Chrissy's epilepsy I rang the paediatrician and he arranged for Chrissy to go back on Epilim.

Ian and I were planning a holiday in Portugal without Chrissy. My sister, Sarah, who was single then, with no children, was upset about our decision.

'She's your flesh and blood. How can you contemplate not taking her with you?' she asked.

Ian did not mince his words in justifying our decision. Previous holidays with Chrissy had not been successful. There was no point in putting her or ourselves through what would be another ordeal. Chrissy could stay in respite, which she enjoyed, and I doubted whether she would be homesick. Chrissy had the capacity then only to take in her current surroundings; she did not refer to time spent elsewhere. Deciding whether to take a child with learning disabilities and challenging behaviour on holiday is a very individual dilemma, not a moral issue. Additional medical problems need to be taken into account, especially if they are not straightforward. Also, special events like birthdays, Christmas and holidays that are enjoyed by most children can evoke different responses in children with challenging behaviour. Chrissy found them overwhelming, even though she wanted to enjoy them.

Sarah has since had two lively, healthy boys and now appreciates the need for respite. She has been on holiday without the children and mum often looks after the boys when she works or goes out socially.

Although I had temporarily given up including Chrissy in our holidays I was idealistic about spending family days together. I loved watching Chrissy's reactions to new experiences. She could be so funny and off-the-wall at times. I took her to a local fête once where a brass band was playing. Suddenly I looked round and realised Chrissy had vanished. Then I noticed a crowd gathering in front of the band. Chrissy had been entertaining them by conducting the bemused musicians. Another time I dressed Chrissy up as a witch for a Hallowe'en party at respite. She really entered into the spirit of it all, making fierce 'witchy' expressions at the camera. She also enjoyed a bonfire party at her school. She loves festive occasions, though they can be a double-edged sword – if Chrissy gets overexcited she can erupt into an outburst. She has little sense of danger either.

Once, we took the children to the local funfair, which Chrissy enjoyed. Ian took her on an unexpectedly fast ride and she tried to throw herself out. He gripped on to her belt for dear life and staggered off the ride looking pale with beads of sweat standing out on his forehead.

'I thought we'd lost her,' he managed to gasp.

Some outings with Chrissy came to a premature and abrupt end. When Ian and I took the children to Whipsnade Zoo, Chrissy played up so badly that we had to come home early, spoiling the day for the other two. And just before Christmas 1992, mum and I took Chrissy, Jamie and Alex to Milton Keynes shopping centre to see their exquisite Christmas village. Once again, the day was in shreds after Chrissy erupted because she could not cope with the queue for Father Christmas. When family outings failed, they failed resoundingly!

Another time, when Chrissy was eight, I took her horse riding and she went into an outburst on the horse. She stripped off and repeated learnt phrases obsessively, like: 'Am I going to respite?' I answered her but she carried on repeating the phrase as if my answer had not sunk in. Then she completely lost control. She lay on the ground and started hurting herself, throwing things, spitting and swearing. Another distressing feature of these outbursts was that she grabbed her crutch and rubbed its secretions across her face, saying: 'Ugh, it smells!' This sometimes happened with faeces as well. I tried to stop her undressing at all costs so she had less access to her nether regions. The following week I decided to give the riding one more shot, and took Chrissy again. This time she was as good as gold!

When Chrissy reached puberty we took her swimming at an outdoor pool. As we sat in the sun, she moved into the shade. I was just unpacking the picnic we had brought with us when Ian muttered: 'Jane, you'd better see to Chrissy.'

I looked round and there she was, sitting in full public view, stroking her breasts with a beatific expression on her face!

We took advantage of coach trips and Christmas parties arranged by various organisations, such as MENCAP and Green Line (a bus company who provided free coaches and drivers), for learning disabled children. On one memorable trip to the seaside Chrissy soiled herself. I cleaned her up and put the mess in a carrier bag. As I walked along the promenade towards the bin, mum (who had come with me) muttered: 'Jane, I hate to tell you, but there's a hole in the bag.' Unfortunately, it was a windy day and as dirty baby wipes blew all over the beach we hastily scurried away from the scene of the crime!

Chrissy particularly enjoyed parties, especially if there was a bouncy castle. Sometimes, if you could see things through the settling-in period, Chrissy would relax and enjoy parties or days out. I found it helpful to have access to a wheelchair, and waterproof protection if rain threatened. But I did not want Chrissy to get too used to being pushed around in a wheelchair in case she came to expect it. If she could get away with not walking she would. Chrissy had a 'thing' about shopping trolleys but convincing her that she was too big to fit in the child's seat was another matter. She also had an embarrassing habit of stimulating herself with the bar between her legs.

For three weeks in the summer holidays that year (1991) Chrissy went to a MENCAP playscheme. Volunteers helped with the children, and they went on lots of outings. It ran from 10am until 3pm, which broke up the long school holiday.

Our holiday in Portugal was a success, though I think many parents would agree that any enjoyment of a holiday or break without the disabled child is tempered by guilt that they are not with you. Chrissy's stay in respite was also a success, though Chrissy had gone into outbursts there where she had mashed things like ice-cream cones and tree bark in her face. At nearly eight, Chrissy's respite allocation was 24 nights a year. I realise that we were lucky. The availability of respite care is patchy throughout the country. Every fortnight Chrissy had tea at their youth club. She was in the habit of wetting every time she arrived for the youth club but she rarely wet herself at home during that period. A psychologist said at a later date that the wetting was a form of attention seeking. But I am not convinced that is the only explanation. Chrissy has an enormous capacity for retaining urine, and I wonder if her nervous system does not always work well enough to convey to her brain that her bladder is full. Sometimes she wet herself when she was vague and disoriented, perhaps in a partial fit.

Even now she was back on Epilim, Chrissy's fits were a problem. It was common for her to have a cluster of fits before a virus or infection came out, even without a high temperature. A fit was often the first sign of an impending infection. Something else I noticed before fits was an increase in difficult behaviour. Her school reported in October 1991 that she had been particularly loud and abusive before having a fit in class. She had a bad cough and I took her to the doctor's. In the car park she had another fit. I held up a queue of cars behind me while I dealt with it. Someone hooted at me and I swore at him. To my embarrassment it was my GP. He leapt out of his car and carried Chrissy into his surgery. He prescribed antibiotics in case she had an infection.

Chrissy's challenging behaviour intensified on antibiotics. Once, after an appalling day with her nagging non-stop and having lots of outbursts, I smacked her. She looked so bewildered, tear-stained and miserable afterwards, I just sat down and cried. I loved, hated and pitied her all at once. It was difficult to know how much she understood about right and wrong. What behaviours was she responsible for and what behaviours were out of her control?

In October 1991 we went back to the genetics clinic at Great Ormond Street Hospital. More blood was taken for chromosome analysis. Again, hope overrode experience. Maybe they would find something this time. As children with learning disabilities grew older, didn't certain changes that come with age help geneticists diagnose them?

CHAPTER 10

Chrissy's Uniqueness

The geneticist told me that he was 99 per cent sure Chrissy had a genetic disorder.

'Unfortunately, Chrissy's set of characteristics are not indicative of a particular syndrome,' he added.

My heart sunk at his words though I could see what he meant. Chrissy is out of synch with the world. Everything about her is off-kilter in some way, as if every cell of her body is affected. Her fine motor co-ordination remains ahead of her gross motor co-ordination. She is loose-jointed, has a high arched palate, sensory problems, epilepsy, small stature, and a slightly unusual face. Her hands are unusual looking too. She could (and does!) bend her fingers right back and her finger pads are tiny.

I love Chrissy's 'flappy' hands. She holds them in odd ways. When she runs she looks like a penguin because her hands stick out by her sides. Odd characteristics are what make us individuals, and Chrissy has plenty of them. I have noticed that she enjoys watching us as much as we enjoy watching her. There seems to be a mutual fascination thing going on. She often has a look of amusement on her face as if she is thinking: 'What on earth are they doing now?' It is almost like Chrissy tries to be human but lacks the necessary tools.

In November 1991 Chrissy was moved into another class at her school with four children who had fallen behind the others. Her teacher admitted that she had not made any progress for a while. Meanwhile, we were very lucky that Jamie's school picked up on his dyslexia. He is bright, and was given remedial teaching from the age of six, so he easily kept up with his classmates. Now you would never know that he had once been labelled 'dyslexic'. Conversely, Chrissy is hyperlexic – her writing skills are above what you would expect from her intellectual ability.

The taxi firm that took Chrissy to school refused to take her in any more because she kept opening windows and doors (where were their child locks?) and disrupting other pupils they transported. I began to take her in and collect her myself. Poor Alex got bitten and attacked a few times in the back of the car during that period.

As Alex got older, her awareness and distress over Chrissy's outbursts grew. They often occurred during the changeover between school and home. She would be tired and irritable, then erupt, often spoiling whatever Alex was doing in the process. Sometimes Alex would call my mum, and if she was in she would come round and take Alex home with her until the outburst was over.

Chrissy's outbursts went through a bizarre stage. She kept complaining about her eyes hurting, though they had not been red or discharging. At home she often wiped her eyes with wet flannels, and they appeared swollen. On other occasions she appeared to have pain in one foot. Her teacher wondered if Chrissy had cramp and, like me, was convinced that these episodes were not just Chrissy being naughty. Often they would happen when Chrissy was doing something she really enjoyed, like drawing. She would screw up or tear the paper and chuck it. Sometimes she would say: 'I sick.' Other times she would shout out 'Go away!' or 'Leave me alone!' as if she could see something I could not. These outbursts lasted up to three hours, but usually around an hour. She could appear to recover in them, then something would flit across her eyes and she would start screaming again. Now she was bigger these outbursts were becoming even more of a problem.

School transport provision had resumed, this time with escorts. One day after school Chrissy's escort turned up at my door looking shaken. Chrissy had been screaming and hurting herself all the way home. At home Chrissy clung to a cushion, screaming: 'Ow! Go away!' and 'My foot hurts!' She kept grabbing her right foot as pain flickered across her face. I tried massaging it but Chrissy was inconsolable. She kept clawing at her face and body and tried to bite me. Then she stripped off, thrashed around on the floor and clawed at her groin. She kept asking for things and when I gave them to her she would throw them. She was absolutely beside herself – and so was I!

This carried on and on until I thought it would only end with medical intervention. I took her down to my local casualty department, where we waited and waited, with Chrissy still frenzied. The casualty nurses' observations were the same as mine, that Chrissy looked as though she was in great pain or discomfort. The casualty doctor sedated her, then suggested I take her home. The doctor came across as frosty and uncaring, when in reality she probably felt as helpless as I when confronted by Chrissy in this state. I mistook her coolness for lack of interest.

'You doctors, you're all the same,' I blew up. 'No one sticks around to observe Chrissy like this. You just come in, take a quick look at her, examine her ears, nose and throat when she lets you. Then say you can find nothing wrong. Of course there's something wrong. Why is she doing this?'

The young doctor burst into tears and left the side room that we had been put in. I sat there feeling ashamed at my angry words. Sometimes it helps us to see that doctors are human too. But then, so are we. When the doctor came back she said that seeing Chrissy like this had been too close to home – her brother had Down's syndrome. I apologised for losing my temper and she offered to write a letter to Chrissy's neurologist about the incident. When we got home I photographed Chrissy's lacerated face and vowed to speak to Chrissy's neurologist myself.

You had to knock Chrissy out completely to stop her outbursts or else let them burn themselves out. Sometimes sedatives seemed to make her over-tired and she would get even worse. It was hit or miss which sedatives worked and in what doses. Sometimes a particular sedative would work, and on another occasion the same sedative would send Chrissy bananas.

I tried holding her tightly in her outbursts, as with 'holding therapy' used on autistic children. Chrissy would arch away from me and scream even louder. The longer I held her, the worse it got. Maybe 'holding' would have eventually stopped the outburst, but with Chrissy's history of such prolonged outbursts I was not hopeful. Also, the point of 'holding' therapy was to induce eye contact and communication in autistic children. Chrissy gave eye contact and communicated to the best of her ability. I found it better just to ride the storm and minimise the damage. Though it would be a lie to claim that I always managed to remain calm and unruffled myself.

I wondered if the outbursts had something to do with epilepsy, but doctors doubted that they were epileptic phenomena as such, though they noted their reciprocal relationship with the fits. Our GP felt that there was a large elective element in Chrissy's outbursts, whilst recognising that behaviour problems are more frequent in children with epilepsy than in the general population. Chrissy's fit frequency was about one a month, but we were suspicious at home and school that she was having absences and subclinical activity, which can manifest as impaired attention and concentration abilities.

When Chrissy was nearly eight, she was assessed at the Wolfson Centre in London. The geneticist at Great Ormond Street had referred her there after being unable to make a specific syndrome diagnosis. A senior registrar and clinical psychologist assessed Chrissy's developmental level with performance tests. She 'performed' well, and I knew they had seen her at her best. They noted that Chrissy had quite a degree of gross motor incoordination – at a three- to four-year level she still came downstairs on her bottom. She had relative strengths in visuo-perceptual skills, but greater difficulty in verbal comprehension and expressive language – below a three-and-a-half-year level. Chrissy's 'delightful' social manner was noted but, summing up, she was assessed as having learning difficulties at a moderate to severe level. The conclusion was that Chrissy would continue to need structured teaching and handling of her behavioural difficulties within a small group. Speech therapy and physiotherapy were also recommended.

Learning the extent of Chrissy's learning difficulties was a shock. I had come to terms with the fact that she'd be a bit backward well before any professionals acknowledged it. Now I gradually became aware that she was going to be far more disabled than I ever imagined. The older she got, the bleaker the future seemed. The teaching staff at Chrissy's school were pessimistic about her development, and so was I. These negative attitudes did not help Chrissy.

We visited a child development centre at Radlett, Hertfordshire, for help with Chrissy's behaviour. We discussed Chrissy's behaviour with her peers and siblings. Chrissy was isolated in the school playground and preferred adult company to children's, often shouting if children got too close. The unprovoked attacks on Alex were put down to her jealousy of Alex overtaking her developmentally. We also discussed Chrissy's hatred of having her hair touched or washed. She often tried urinating in the bath to prevent me washing her hair!

A child psychologist at the centre noted that time out did not work with Chrissy. She wanted to try positively rewarding good behaviour and ignoring bad. I had to keep a behaviour diary. It would have saved time if I had thought to keep a behaviour diary for a few weeks before the appointment. It helped to put the outbursts into perspective and appreciate the times when Chrissy was calm. Sometimes, a pattern of behaviour can be revealed by keeping a behaviour diary, but no real pattern emerged with Chrissy. However, more triggers were detected.

Chrissy responded well to praise but it was difficult to ignore destructive challenging behaviour, especially when we were out. Chrissy's progress was also hampered by her seemingly having no recollection of previous consequences to a specific behaviour. Her short-term memory and expressive language were poor, so we were in for a long haul using this particular behavioural approach.

On the positive side, the development centre's staff, like those at the Wolfson Centre before, praised Chrissy's social manner, noting that Chrissy was a 'delightful little girl with a great deal of potential'. Soon afterwards our ear, nose and throat surgeon also gave Chrissy a similar compliment. I felt proud of her and it made me all the more determined to reduce the negative behaviours that threatened to drown her positive qualities.

The first time I heard that Chrissy might have to leave school was during a home visit from the psychologist in October 1992. The school was no longer able to meet Chrissy's needs. If Chrissy did not have challenging behaviour alongside her borderline moderate to severe learning disabilities, she might have been able to cope at an MLD (moderate learning difficulties) school. As it was, the challenging behaviour sealed her fate.

I attended a meeting at the school with Chrissy's teacher, a speech therapist and an educational psychologist. The picture the school painted was depressing and I felt that the educational psychologist was completely uninformed about Chrissy's needs. Teaching staff gave the impression that Chrissy's behaviour was worse at school than at home. It was all doom and gloom and the educational psychologist suggested a weekly boarding school. He said that the school had only 14 pupils and a high staff–pupil ratio. I was told that the pupils all had learning and behaviour problems. The educational psychologist's view was that Chrissy needed 24-hour care to modify her behaviour. I was prepared to look at the school – he made it sound ideal for Chrissy's needs. But did anyone involved in this meeting about Chrissy's future have any idea what her needs were?

CHAPTER 11

Changes for Chrissy, Changes for Me

As soon as the boarding school's head started asking Chrissy questions, I knew we should not have been there. The deputy head had visited Chrissy at her current school yet he did not seem to know that Chrissy had learning disabilities or epilepsy. I saw only a few pupils, but it soon became apparent that they were disruptive and behaviourally disturbed rather than learning disabled.

I was livid that so many people had got it wrong. It was as if they could not give a toss where Chrissy ended up, as long as she did not stay at her current school. The explanation infuriated me further, though Chrissy's teacher apologised profusely.

'Because the cause of Chrissy's problems is unknown the local education authorities haven't got "mental handicap" on Chrissy's file,' she explained.

This further underlines my assertions about the usefulness of having a diagnosis. And what about the educational psychologist, deputy head and all the other professionals involved in Chrissy's move? A wrongly labelled file was no excuse.

Two more suggestions were made – both SLD (severe learning difficulties) schools. One was local and the other about six miles away. When I looked at the one furthest away, the pupils appeared more able than those at the local school, despite the schools both being in the same educational needs category. The authorities would not fund transport or support a move for Chrissy to the furthest one, so I looked more closely at the local one – Woodfield School, Hemel Hempstead.

The facilities were excellent. They had an indoor swimming pool and a sensory room. The staff were committed and the mood upbeat. However, there were many children with profound learning disabilities. Chrissy had met many of them at MENCAP parties and outings, and I wondered how she would fit in. After all, she was not *that* disabled. It seemed like another step down, more lowering of my expectations. Would Chrissy be better off struggling at the bottom of the class, but with higher demands made on her, or would she gain valuable self-esteem by being one of the more able pupils?

The school's head reassured me that pupils were taught at levels appropriate to their individual needs. There were other pupils like Chrissy with borderline moderate/severe learning disabilities whose behaviour tipped the balance against an MLD school. There was a higher staff to pupil ratio too. I felt more and more relieved as the head spoke about what the school could offer Chrissy. What swung it for me completely was the school's positive attitude about their pupils. Their teaching staff remarked on the negativity of the previous school's report about Chrissy. It highlighted all her shortcomings, and only paid lip service to her abilities and achievements.

'We want to focus on what Chrissy *can* do,' the head stated, explaining the reward and reinforcement systems the school used for good behaviour and achievements. 'We believe in letting the children have as many choices as possible.'

I spoke about the problems we had taking Chrissy out into the community, and felt encouraged by the school's aims to help the children mix by taking them shopping and involving them in other community-based activities. I took Chrissy on several visits to her new school before she started full-time there in the spring of 1993. Teaching staff had tried not to base their expectations on the report from the previous school but, even so, they were pleasantly surprised by how well she settled in.

I must emphasise here that Chrissy's previous school had not been a negative experience throughout for us. We have some lovely memories of Chrissy's early years there, and she had some caring teachers. She was encouraged to take part in their sports days, and we enjoyed social events like their yearly bonfire night parties. The negativity only became apparent towards the end of Chrissy's time there. The other children in her small subgroup were moved too. Some parents believed that their children were pawns in a bigger political picture. The school did not usually take children with such complex and severe difficulties. They had no involvement with MENCAP, for example. We believed that they had taken children like Chrissy on because they needed to keep their numbers up when they had been threatened with closure and an amalgamation with another MLD school. Once that threat had ended our children were superfluous to requirements.

I felt bitter that Chrissy had been used in this way. The school's head had promised me faithfully that while he was still in office Chrissy would not be moved. However, it all turned out for the best. Chrissy improved at her new school and I felt that they had her best interests as an individual at heart, not just the school's.

When Chrissy turned nine Ian bought her a watch and I made her a clock birthday cake. She was learning all about time at school and it had become another fixation. Any new skill she acquired threw up a new set of difficulties to overcome.

'What's the time?' she would ask a hundred times a day! Answering Chrissy's repetitive questions did not help. She would go on and on without processing my responses. I discussed this at a meeting with the school's speech therapist.

'Chrissy's unusual in that her expressive language is greater than her comprehension,' the speech therapist said. 'She's inconsistent too, understanding something one day, then not the next.'

We discussed how Chrissy's behaviour hindered her progress. The speech therapist felt that Chrissy was frightened by her own lack of control.

I do not know how much Chrissy's hearing loss contributed to her poor comprehension skills. She continued to have problems with her ears. Frequently, ear infections were preceded by fits. I knew that Chrissy had auras before her fits because she sought out an adult just before one came on. What her experience of an aura was I do not know. I have read and heard about other people with epilepsy saying that they feel odd sensations, like *déjà vu*, euphoria, fright, or impending doom. Hearing, vision, taste and sense of smell can also be affected. Chrissy would say 'I feel sick' and often look quite panic-stricken before succumbing to the seizure. I do not know what caused the fear: whether it was knowledge of the impending fit or just a feeling that something bad was going to happen. Even though the fits themselves were only about one or two minutes long, Chrissy was exhausted afterwards. She would sleep for about two hours, then wake up subdued.

Chrissy's neurologist doubted that epilepsy was involved in Chrissy's outbursts but he upped the Epilim dosage and arranged for another EEG. The EEG recording showed nothing new, just confirmation that Chrissy had epilepsy. No focus for the fits was found. We often appeared to have honeymoon periods after anticonvulsants were increased, but they did not last long. I wondered if Chrissy's body got used to the higher levels.

Was Epilim causing her weight gain? Chrissy did not eat much but she was ballooning into a little butterball. It was getting increasingly hard to find clothes for her because she was so short and with this huge belly. Because of her size Chrissy was getting harder to handle. I considered getting a large buggy-type pushchair for her and discovered by contacting social services that they could loan me one. Though it took a while to come through.

During term time I just about managed to cope with Chrissy's outbursts; but during school holidays everything fell apart, despite respite breaks. My diary notes for one day in the 1993 Easter holidays reads:

> Chrissy won't leave Alex alone. She's repetitive 'screamy' and destructive. She's just wrecked Ian's camera flash. I'm fed up with the responsibility. It's like a bloody treadmill.

I feel sad when I read notes like that because I realise how caught up I was in the downside of having a learning disabled child with challenging behaviour. The minutiae of day-to-day life ground me down and I had no time to stop and consider Chrissy's good points.

The trouble is, when you are fighting to keep your head above water you do not have time to look at the scenery.

Chrissy's disability had ruled my life for eight years and given me an identity. It was too easy to hide behind it and become obsessed with fighting battles for her to the exclusion of all else. I started looking for something to do outside the family. Relying on Ian and my disability benefits to support us did nothing for my self-esteem. I harboured secret ambitions to write short stories for magazines. I had written diaries for years and enjoyed writing letters too, so I enrolled on a creative writing course. I also looked for other work that I could do around the children.

I started off doing part-time sales work. I worked for commission only doing sales parties in people's homes and distributing catalogues. It involved too much work for peanuts, but I had no idea what I wanted to do in the long term. I even tried care work, looking after a patient at the environmental clinic where my sister worked. Emptying the patient's commode turned my stomach. Somehow, I just did not have the touch. I felt restricted about going back into an office and using my secretarial skills – I knew nothing about computers and word processors. One solution was to do a mainly home-based course for a new career. I sent off for some Open University course information, and decided to go on their 'Women Back to Work' course. It helped me to focus on what skills I had and what I wanted to do. As part of the course I put together quite a presentable CV. It is amazing how some skills mums gain running a family can transfer to a CV.

In May 1992 I went for an interview at Cell Barnes, St Albans, which was a hospital for learning disabled adults; for some of them it was the only home they had ever known. The hospital wanted a medical secretary to work ten hours a week. Because of my computer illiteracy, I did not expect to get the job. But I thought the interview would be good experience. I was also sceptical about how I would manage to get childcare.

'I don't know why I bothered going for the job,' I confided in a friend with four children. 'Even if I got it I couldn't manage in the school holidays.'

'Just go for the job and worry about childcare afterwards,' my friend advised.

To my delight and amazement, I was offered the job. It was to cover for someone on sick leave. Luckily, mum offered to look after the children during the school holidays because the hours were so few. I still did my sales job, and it was a challenge to combine the two jobs, my coursework, and my family.

The secretarial job at the hospital was right up my street. I attended lectures on specific syndromes and wrote up residents' case notes. Another secretary there taught me how to use the word processor. I wondered how I had ever managed with a typewriter! I was chuffed to bits at my new-found skills. Their medical library was another bonus and they allowed me to take books home. When the lady on sick leave returned I got further agency work as a medical secretary, both there and in different departments at my local hospital in Hemel Hempstead. I only worked in term time when the children were at school. Much of my work involved wading through piles of medical notes and listening to stacks of audio-tapes. I needed reference books for some medical terms that I had never heard of. At times it was like listening to a foreign language.

Learning about other syndromes and conditions made me wonder about Chrissy's mortality. Not having a diagnosis meant that I had no idea whether her particular condition would be life limiting. Some of the more profoundly disabled children I met through Contact '81 had died young. Two boys from the same family died from their degenerative conditions. Another boy with a life-limiting disability died, and tragically a year later his mother lost her other child in a car accident. As time passes I hear about other untimely deaths and my heart goes out to the parents.

Some people still harbour views that our children do not have much quality of life so they are more dispensable than non-disabled children. I can honestly say that losing Chrissy would be as shattering as losing either of my other children. I am lucky that she has no congenital organ defects and is comparatively healthy.

CHAPTER 12

Two Steps Forward, Three Steps Back

Chrissy and I both made new friends through her new school. Another mum of a learning disabled boy was going through the same process as I had the previous year. She too had been told that her son's MLD school could no longer meet his needs, and she wanted reassurance about the one Chrissy moved to. She had a different attitude to her son's disabilities than I had to Chrissy's. She was very laid back and had no idea what was wrong with him. I nagged her to get some tests done and informed her about disability benefits. Like me, she had been in the dark until she met another parent. She took her son to Great Ormond Street Hospital for tests but, like Chrissy's, they came back showing no known cause for his disabilities. He ended up in the same class as Chrissy at school. Sports days at the SLD school were very different from those at the MLD one. There were no competitive events because it would not be feasible. Various activities were set up and the children worked their way round each one. Chrissy was great at welly throwing!

Chrissy was still isolated in many ways and did not like other children invading her space. At best, she tolerated her peers rather than interacting with them. Chrissy became fascinated by babies. It was a new development that I noticed when a friend brought her baby round to meet the children. Chrissy kept bringing her doll down to 'mother' it as she saw adults do with the baby.

There were small improvements in Chrissy's general behaviour (in between the outbursts). I took her to the circus and she was in her element, clapping and dancing in her seat. I get such pleasure from watching her having fun. Chrissy's whole face lights up and her body vibrates with joy. Every small improvement was a cause for celebration. Chrissy managed to help me shell peas and lay the table for dinner one night. Her manual dexterity allowed her to do such tasks, but her concentration span and volatility often prevented her from complying.

In August 1993 Ian and I took Jamie and Alex to France on holiday while Chrissy went on another MENCAP holiday. During some of our time away, Chrissy had an unsuccessful stay in respite with lots of wetting and screaming. She had been through a difficult spell before we went away so we could not be sure why she had behaved badly. Respite staff said that she frequently asked about us, but then she nags 'Am I going to respite?' when she is with us. Once again, it was hard to pin behavioural changes on anything in particular. It did not stop me feeling guilty though, wondering if she had missed us.

I asked our link-worker at respite to write something down about Chrissy's behaviour there so I could take it on our next visit to Great Ormond Street Hospital. I decided to keep another behavioural diary too. Chrissy's outbursts continued after she came home; then, like the sun coming out, we had a run of wonderful days. Unfortunately, they were followed a week later by more outbursts.

In November 1993 Chrissy's neurologist suggested weaning Chrissy off her Epilim. After each reduction, Chrissy's behaviour worsened. I was terribly confused. Her behaviour got worse when Epilim was increased, yet now it was getting worse as it decreased. What on earth was happening? School reported that Chrissy was having prolonged outbursts that she was unable to calm down from. She was wetting herself frequently too.

The outbursts were like the ones she had experienced previously where she complained of physical pains, claiming that her head, tummy, teeth and eyes hurt. Most of the pain seemed to be focused around her eyes; and, as before, she often clawed at them and rubbed at them with wet flannels. When Chrissy complained that her eyes hurt it was like a warning sign, heralding an impending outburst. The school doctor, Janet Hislop, who was also a consultant paediatrician, listened, sympathetically, as I described Chrissy's outbursts to her at a school medical. She felt that a 24-hour EEG would be beneficial in case there was an epileptic component in them. She wrote to the neurologist for me, and the school lent me their video camera to record an outburst. I felt that things were moving at last. They could not carry on as they were. Not knowing what mood Chrissy would wake up in, come home from school in or change from in a split second made me feel powerless.

By the Christmas holidays in 1993 I was desperate. My GP had given me sedatives for Chrissy, but they did not seem to be working. I was frightened of my angry feelings towards her. I liken it to having a baby who will not stop crying. If you have done everything possible to soothe the baby yet it still cries you go down the garden and take deep breaths, or turn up the stereo to drown out the noise. I could not do that with Chrissy. She was too destructive, both to herself and to property. I made an emergency appointment at our local surgery. Chrissy had an outburst there that left me trembling.

Patients are given numbered cards to indicate their place in the queue. As each doctor becomes free, the doctor's name lights up on a screen in the waiting room. Chrissy was riveted by the whole procedure.

'What's the number?' she questioned me, obsessively, getting increasingly distraught. 'What number's the doctor?'

It went on and on, despite my attempts to distract her with the books and toys there. She completely exploded and everyone in the waiting room stared as I tried to prevent her stripping off. I had to carry her into the doctor's room – no mean feat. Chrissy weighed about six stone then. The doctor suggested upping her sedative. When I got home I rang the community mental handicap team (CMHT). Thankfully, they were able to arrange for Chrissy to go into respite care for the day. Episodes like that were shattering experiences. It is hard to explain how caught up I get in them. I found it hard to remain calm whilst physically restraining Chrissy on my own. All my emotions were in turmoil too.

Upping the sedative and Chrissy spending a day in respite were holding measures, like all the others we had used so far; they did not address the fundamental problem.

The following day, Christmas Eve, I called the doctor out during a similar outburst that went on and on. There was no way I was going through the ordeal at the surgery again. Chrissy was bruised and lacerated. Mum was available that day to help, and we took turns to hold Chrissy's arms down to stop her hurting herself. The doctor prescribed a different sedative, Largactil, which appeared to work in a larger dose. (Previously, in small doses, it seemed to make Chrissy worse.) Largactil worked but Chrissy looked pitiful afterwards, pale and sleepy. Even when calm, she complained, groggily, that she felt sick and the area around her face hurt. As soon as she recovered, she had another outburst and so it went on over Christmas. Chrissy was either distressed or sleepy.

The cycle broke when we went to Newcastle-under-Lyme to visit Ian's parents over New Year. I slept and slept, as I often did when we went there. Ian's mum is brilliant at occupying the children, and Ian and I were grateful for the respite. We were having more than our fair share of arguments because we were both so tense much of the time. Because we both had so much to do (Ian's work is very demanding) it was easy to put our relationship last. We would snap at each other over silly things, though we never let the sun go down on a row. Time away was the only chance we had to get to know and appreciate each other as people again.

I realise that some parents do not get any breaks. And I have no idea how they cope. Despite respite, and despite more and more professionals becoming aware of Chrissy, we were finding it increasingly difficult to manage. I could have decreased my workload, but that would have created more problems than it solved. Working was an escape from Chrissy's problems.

I gave up my sales job when a better opportunity beckoned, and became a self-employed jewellery distributor after seeing some beautiful costume jewellery at a house party. I could still work around the children, and it gave me the opportunity of building my own business. My supplier was an innovative multi-level marketing company that gave independent distributors opportunities to earn commissions both on their own sales and on those of sales people they introduced. I loved the product and enjoyed the inspiring training meetings. As I built up my sales teams I wrote regular newsletters, offering incentives and giving tips on improving sales and team building. I used my creativity to the full and it boosted my confidence no end. It was great that I could run it from home, and it was an exciting time because I believed that my business would be a success.

However, the company was not without teething problems. Items were out of stock and deliveries were incomplete. I had to deal with my own customers and reassure my sales team. It was my first experience of running a business and I could not have done it without Ian's help. He advised me, kept my feet on the ground and did my accounts. I felt driven by this new venture and, at times, exhausted. Whatever I do I throw myself into it wholeheartedly! However, because I was so tired and work brought different stresses into my life, when Chrissy played up I found it physically harder to cope.

I was still having problems with heavy periods. And sticking to a keep-fit regime was not enough to keep my back problems at bay. When my back seized up I took painkillers and carried on. I should have seen the signs and realised that we were in danger of approaching another breaking point. But when you are in the thick of it, the waters are muddied, and it is hard to see the situation clearly.

CHAPTER 13

Behaviour versus Epilepsy

I gave Chrissy regular sedatives when she erupted. But they took a while to work and only delayed the inevitable. If she was going to have an outburst she would have one when the sedative wore off. I felt very unhappy about the situation, and hoped that our next visit to Great Ormond Street Hospital would prove fruitful. I had gathered information and managed to video an outburst. Respite and school staff wrote notes about their experiences with Chrissy for me to take to the hospital. I was determined that we were not going to be fobbed off with more sedatives and anticonvulsants. I wanted to know what caused these episodes.

In January 1994 Chrissy was admitted to Great Ormond Street Hospital the night before she was booked in for a magnetic resonance imaging (MRI) scan. A general anaesthetic was arranged because she would not have co-operated for the scan. During her first night there she woke up and wet herself during a prolonged outburst. In the morning she was sedated prior to the general anaesthetic. She woke up when she was moved from her ward into the scanning room and promptly went into another full-blown outburst. It was incredibly violent. She bashed her head against the metal bars of her bed, and tore at herself. I was relieved that at last someone was able to observe her in a major outburst. But I was in for a crushing disappointment.

The nurses were shocked at Chrissy's distress. One nurse, who had worked in child psychiatry, said that she had seen children with mental health problems in tantrums before, but this was something else. Normally, they gave up when they were tired but Chrissy's outbursts went beyond that. The neurologist was called to the ward. He appeared, flanked by junior doctors, took one look at Chrissy, who was writhing around on the floor, and said: 'That's behaviour.'

I immediately went on the offensive. I believed that if he thought the outbursts were purely behavioural then he considered them as being in her control, purely a means of manipulating her surroundings. I had become increasingly defensive about health professionals' claims that Chrissy's outbursts were behavioural. I knew that Chrissy had tantrums and behavioural outbursts too and agreed that the prolonged outbursts were not purely epileptic in nature. However, I was convinced that there was some unknown epileptic component in them because they were so unrelenting. Chrissy's teachers and school nurse had also expressed their suspicions that epilepsy was behind the prolonged outbursts because of the way something would just come over her when she was sitting doing something she enjoyed. Also, they had seen her desperate attempts at self control. 'I want to be good,' she would sob, then she would fling herself on the floor and bang her head or start biting her hands.

I threw questions at the neurologist like darts: 'If it's behavioural, then how come she's had these from infancy? Why does she wake up in the night like this? Why doesn't any intervention stop them? Why are there often no triggers and why are they self-limiting? Why are they cyclic, and worse in late afternoon? What about the strange physical symptoms – the sore eyes, the pains in her face and extremities? And what's causing the paranoia and apparent delusions? What about the reciprocal relationship with the fits?'

Not surprisingly, the neurologist was taken aback. When my emotions are stirred up I am hopeless at putting my point over rationally. The neurologist's answers did not satisfy me.

'What we're seeing now probably isn't the same as those you saw when she was a baby. This doesn't look like any fit that I've seen. Epileptic episodes don't last as long as this. Drugs won't stop these – they're behavioural.'

I stormed off the ward and had a good cry. I felt so frustrated to have come this far yet still have no answers. When I returned the neurologist wanted to talk to me. He retracted what he had said about drugs and suggested a new anticonvulsant – gabapentin.

'I doubt that what I observed is caused by epileptic activity, but I agree that there appears to be a reciprocal relationship between the fits and the behavioural outbursts. We'll re-establish links with the child development centre, and see her again here in a month. Meanwhile, keep a behaviour diary,' he advised.

Later on that day, Ian came to see Chrissy in hospital. He put his views over in a calmer and more concise way than I had. The neurologist admitted that he did not know what these outbursts were. He said that behaviour sometimes worsened in children with epilepsy when fits were well controlled. He also said that he would consult their psychiatrist. The psychiatrist was interested in the hallucinatory component of Chrissy's outbursts. He then had a discussion with the neurologist about what drugs to try to control the behavioural problems; some psychiatric drugs should not be taken by people with epilepsy. They decided to go with the neurologist's plan and review the situation in a month.

Chrissy stayed another night because, when they had finally managed to anaesthetise her for the MRI scan, she was difficult to rouse afterwards, and the doctors needed to see her fully alert after the anaesthetic before allowing her home. The next night (at home) Chrissy slept through the night for the first time in weeks. Two days later, the first thing I noticed when she came in from school was her smiley face and pink cheeks. (She looks pale and wretched when she is going through a bad phase.) I asked her for a kiss. 'Screaming's gone,' she said.

Chrissy's teacher reported that she had been 'brilliant', amenable and well behaved. I felt ridiculously emotional. Yet it could not be the gabapentin, it had only been started four days before. Maybe it was the general anaesthetic or all the sedation. Probably it was just Chrissy's emergence from another bad cycle of outbursts. As always, I was foolishly optimistic. I rang friends and family to tell them about the change in Chrissy. They all warned me gently: 'Don't count your chickens…'

I rang the drug company that makes gabapentin. They said that it does enter the system quickly, but they did not know how long it would take to reach the brain. They were very interested in Chrissy because the use of gabapentin in children was so new. I gave them details of Chrissy's neurologist so that they could monitor her progress.

This honeymoon period did not last. Chrissy had an epileptic fit within a week of gabapentin's introduction. Then the usual ups and downs began again. There was a long gap overnight without any drugs, so I redistributed the doses so that they were more evenly spaced. The next day Chrissy had three violent, unrelenting out bursts. I phoned the neurologist, who suggested upping the dose. The next day Chrissy was fine, but the day after was abysmal. Her school reported that she had been out of control; and after school she had screamed non-stop at home. Chrissy's social worker visited in the midst of it all and was completely nonplussed. Alex played up too. It was hardly surprising. After all, she saw an apparently naughty child getting cuddles rather than admonishment. I needed firm strategies to deal with these outbursts – difficult when we did not know what caused them. I gave Chrissy more Largactil and rang the neurologist again. He was away. All these drugs, and no lasting change had been effected.

Chrissy's epileptic 'absences' became more frequent, though her major fits still occurred roughly once a month. I noted, when Chrissy had a fit outside my local post office, how people rally round when someone is obviously 'ill'. I had offers of tissues, cups of water and chairs. Yet everyone gives me a wide berth when Chrissy is in an outburst. I had heard about a hospital for children that specialised in epilepsy and behavioural disorders. They assess and monitor children, then stabilise them on drugs. If Chrissy did not improve I would try to get her seen there.

However, once again, Chrissy turned around. She was wonderful, full of smiles and mischief. It lasted a few days. Then she started having night-time outbursts again. Coupled with these were daytime absences. She kept getting sleepy at school. At home she would complain that her eyes hurt, then become vague, disoriented and unsteady on her feet.

All I wanted was for her to have some peace, an end to her suffering. I felt a sense of impending doom.

CHAPTER 14

Ups and Downs

Absences and outbursts that Chrissy could not get out of continued at school and at home. I took the girls shopping in Hemel Hempstead one day when Chrissy seemed calm. She had an outburst in a department store. Poor Alex, then only five, had to carry Chrissy's shoes and my bags while I carried Chrissy back to the car. I thanked God for my disabled badge at times like this. I sedated Chrissy with Largactil when she still carried on after we got home. She had made her nose bleed and thrown a plant, so there was mess everywhere. Chrissy had recovered by the evening. She danced the night away at a respite care disco as if she hadn't a care in the world.

Apart from that incident and a few more ups and downs, Chrissy seemed markedly better in the days before our follow-up visit to Great Ormond Street Hospital. When we arrived at the hospital Chrissy played happily in the waiting area. Then she complained that her eyes hurt and had an absence, followed by a ten-minute outburst. By the time the neurologist saw her she had calmed down completely. She accepted his examination and was responsive and sweet.

He looked at her speculatively and said: 'I've never seen her calm like this.'

He remarked upon Chrissy's 'unusual elfin face', then went on to talk about gabapentin. He said that, out of the three new anti-convulsants they were using on children, gabapentin had so far proved the most successful, and he felt that we should continue it. We discussed the results of the MRI scan. Only the left sensory neural deafness showed up. The most recent EEG showed typical 'absence waves'. I asked about 24-hour EEGs, and the neurologist said that would be their next step if Chrissy deteriorated further.

Chrissy gained weight, an unfortunate side-effect of many anti-convulsants, but that eventually stabilised. Her behaviour improved, but continued to vary widely. Her prolonged outbursts occurred about twice weekly. At our next visit to Great Ormond Street the neurologist said that he did not think Chrissy would come to any real harm in them, and felt that they should be allowed to abate themselves. If, however, they were particularly distressing, he recommended a diazepam (Valium) injection. As I have already said, Valium had an adverse effect on Chrissy.

The psychiatrist suggested propranolol because he felt that Chrissy's visual disturbances and distress might be caused by childhood migraine. He also felt that regular doses of chlorpromazine would be helpful. Once again I went off in search of information. This time I looked up everything I could find on migraine. I could see why it had been considered, but propranolol, like everything else we had tried, made no difference to the outbursts.

Chrissy's medical needs still were not being met, but her educational ones were. At her school review she came in to show me her book of achievement. It was delightful – with photos of Chrissy and schoolwork she had done. Chrissy's face was wreathed in smiles as we went through it.

In March 1994 Chrissy had a nasty accident at respite. I was relieved that I was at work, which left poor Ian to deal with it. She had tripped over a step on a visit to the local fire station, and cut her lip. Her tooth was chipped too. She had to go to the casualty department at our local hospital for stitches. Apparently she was hysterical. Her dentist saw her the following day and said she would have to have the tooth capped under a general anaesthetic. Here we go again!

Over Easter 1994 Chrissy went with a group on a pilgrimage to Lourdes for a week. I was not hoping for miracles, just a break. When we picked Chrissy up at Gatwick after her trip, she was beaming. Jamie and Alex flanked her protectively. It was a moment to remember, but unfortunately I did not have my camera. A month later the Lourdes trip organisers arranged a reunion picnic at a park in Twickenham. It was a beautiful, cloudless day, and the children had a wonderful time playing cricket and running about.

Jamie began to seem happier about spending time with us, though his behaviour varied as widely as Chrissy's. He tested us to the limits. He was always lively and needed lots of entertaining. But sometimes he was loving and sweet; at other times he was uncontrollable, aggressive and disruptive. It was hard to set boundaries when he was going back to his dad's, who found it hard to stick to them. If I got angry or tried to instil discipline, Jamie would become abusive, and phone his dad to pick him up. It was a no-win situation. Jamie played us off, one against the other, and it took us time to figure out how to work together in such instances.

Jamie's visits often ended on a sour note. There were even times when I wondered whether contact with me disturbed him to the point where it was unhealthy to carry on trying to force it. But not seeing him for any length of time was like having a limb cut off. Either one of us would make the first move to re-establish our relationship after he had gone off in a huff, swearing (literally!) never to visit again. It illustrates my point in the introduction: no matter how abhorrent certain behaviours are, your love for your child remains undiminished.

I often agonised over whether I could have handled any given situation better and I made contingency plans should that particular behaviour recur. However, I find that children with difficult behaviour are often one step ahead. You get a handle on a particular behaviour, figure out how to deal with it, then another one pops up in its place.

On the rare occasions that the three children played happily and quietly together I remarked upon it. I was one of three, and am well aware of how much siblings quarrel and fight; but interactions involving Chrissy and Jamie were far more extreme and intractable. And they did not improve with age. Alex was sandwiched between her demanding brother and sister. Ian and I have done our utmost to minimise any adverse effects on her, whilst trying to help the other two, and I think so far we've succeeded. She is happy and confident. She achieves at school, both in sport and academically, and enjoys her busy life. I was, and still am, idealistic about happy families. It is only when the children are all safe in their beds under my roof that I can allow myself the luxury of feeling content that we are all together.

However, even at night there were nasty surprises. One night when Chrissy was ten I heard her cry out about two hours after she had gone to bed. I thought it would lead into a prolonged outburst like it usually did. But instead, when I flew upstairs, Chrissy was walking unsteadily round in ever-decreasing circles, looking terrified. I recognised from her glazed eyes that she was going into a fit. From that time onwards Chrissy's fits were mainly nocturnal. Her epilepsy became an unseen enemy that crept up on her and struck when she was at her most vulnerable.

Many of her daytime fits had started with her suddenly needing to go to sleep, then waking from sleep to go into the fit. This was the same type of fit, short-lived, but exhausting Chrissy afterwards. The only difference was that Chrissy sometimes came out of the nocturnal fits in an altered state of awareness, smacking her lips and plucking at her covers. She would mumble nonsense and her movements would be repetitive and purposeless – automatisms. I knew from the books that I had read on epilepsy that these were complex partial seizures. Automatic behaviour can occur on its own in such fits, or as part of a major seizure. Because Chrissy had an aura before her fits it meant that they were not generalised seizures. They started at a focus, then spread across her brain.

The reciprocal relationship between fits and outbursts had diminished. Either could appear at any time, though the outbursts still tended to come in cycles. Chrissy's eyes still bothered her a lot at times and she complained of seeing 'funny lights'.

In June 1994 I received a letter from Great Ormond Street Hospital, suggesting that we try phenytoin again, the anticonvulsant Chrissy was on when she was a toddler. I remembered how sleepy it had made her, and felt uneasy. Chrissy's reactions were unpredictable and extreme at times. I'd had enough of conducting drug trials at home and did not feel that they were fair on Chrissy either.

CHAPTER 15

In-patient Assessment

What had happened to the 24-hour EEG (ambulatory monitoring) Chrissy's neurologist had mentioned? I was told that they did not have the facilities at Great Ormond Street. I asked my GP for a second opinion. Janet Hislop, Chrissy's school doctor, had suggested the children's hospital I'd heard about in Oxford. My GP refused, saying that it would be too costly. I appreciated that, by now, Chrissy had cost the NHS a great deal of money. But so far no one had been able to help her enough to give her any quality of life.

'Chrissy is not our only patient, you know,' my GP explained. 'There are other people more needy than her and we can only provide so much funding.'

He made me feel greedy and inconsiderate. But the bottom line was that Chrissy was my child and my concern at that time was for her, not for other patients in the practice. I approached the local health authority, but they argued that Chrissy could get what she needed medically in Hertfordshire. There was nowhere in the county that Chrissy could have gone for in-patient assessment. So I went to the local press to plead my case. It was successful. The health authority agreed to funding.

Chrissy spent two months at The Park Hospital for Children in Oxford after admission in December 1994. She attended their school and we brought her home over Christmas and every weekend. The key issues that the hospital hoped to address were the contribution of the epilepsy to Chrissy's learning difficulties and challenging behaviour. There was also an opportunity to assess Chrissy's behaviour and the effects of various interventions.

Many types of behaviour are addressed there. Some children I saw were autistic or had other learning disabilities and behaviour problems. Others were victims of deprived backgrounds. The cycle of abuse was brought home to me when an older nurse told me: 'It's terribly sad – we see children here whose parents were also here when they were young.'

I spent a week there to help keep the electrodes on while Chrissy had ambulatory monitoring, which was technically very difficult because she screamed and struggled throughout the recordings.

Observations about Chrissy's behaviour were interesting. The nursing staff noted that Chrissy needed to be given instructions with very few words and very clear limits set. Ignoring her was not usually effective, as she worked herself up into a tantrum, which was then difficult to break. As she increased her efforts at gaining attention her self-control diminished, which could lead to prolonged episodes of screaming and self-injurious behaviour. Chrissy's teacher there said that, despite Chrissy's loud and challenging behaviour, she was likeable with a good sense of fun. She remarked on Chrissy's intolerance of her peers. If anyone else got attention Chrissy shouted loudly. In group situations Chrissy found it hard to concentrate, and demanded attention by going through her repertoire of learnt phrases or asking irrelevant questions. The teacher noted that Chrissy had no understanding of the need to defer or modify the immediate satisfaction of her wishes.

Teaching staff experienced the same difficulties as I had with transitions. Giving her prior warning beforehand helped. The teacher reiterated the nursing staff's views that Chrissy needed short, simple instructions which she should be encouraged to repeat to ensure she understood what was expected of her. Time on the computer (Chrissy's favourite activity then) was used in school as a reward. Chrissy was able to concentrate for half an hour on simple programs devised for pre-schoolers.

The gabapentin was gradually withdrawn so that EEG recordings could be done before and after reduction of anticonvulsant medication. Paroxysms were either generalised or limited to the left hemisphere of the brain. No correlation between Chrissy's behaviour and EEG changes was observed. Even the absence-like episodes were not associated with any EEG change. Either the EEG recordings were not foolproof indicators of epilepsy, or Chrissy's 'absences' or specific behaviour changes were due to something else.

Chrissy's consultant acknowledged that some brain activity limited to deep cortical structures may not produce effects detectable by an EEG. But she concluded that those behaviours I had suspected were epileptic were unlikely to be, because many of the episodes lasted for several minutes and any alteration in consciousness during that period would have shown on the EEG. I was surprised because I had always believed that Chrissy's epilepsy had a far more detrimental effect on her life than the EEGs had indicated.

Chrissy's consultant conceded Chrissy's potential for epilepsy, and an increase in epileptiform brain activity after withdrawal of gabapentin made her consider maintaining Chrissy on gabapentin. She felt that Chrissy's epilepsy, if left uncontrolled, would affect both her learning, especially information processing, and cortical maturation.

Chrissy's consultant noted that the frequency of behavioural problems is inversely correlated with the level of an individual's cognitive functioning – their understanding. Although Chrissy's vocabulary appears to be adequate, she has limited abstract expression (e.g. she finds it hard to communicate on the telephone as she has no visual clues to understand what the other person is saying) and therefore has difficulty communicating her emotional state and experience of pain.

Chrissy's limited information processing may also explain her reluctance for change. Sudden environmental change may surprise and panic her because she does not have the ability to process rapidly what is happening around her. This in turn may precipitate behavioural difficulties. Chrissy's obsessive traits and preoccupations provide her with control and routine, enabling her to cope better with her environment. Structure and predictability are functionally very important to her. Overloading her with stimuli (e.g. too much verbal information, too many people or too much choice) results in increased anxiety because she will not be able to cope with those demands.

The staff at Oxford appreciated Chrissy's sense of humour and fun, but they found her exhausting, demanding constant one-to-one attention. In the consultant's opinion, outbursts appear to serve two main functions: access to reinforcing outcomes and a communicative act. The majority of observed and recorded behaviours at the hospital were followed by increased adult attention. They credited Ian and me for coping well at home with Chrissy, because the unstructured home environment is the most difficult place to look after children like Chrissy.

Chrissy was also seen by a geneticist there, who raised the question of Smith–Magenis syndrome (SMS), which is associated with a deletion on chromosome 17. The syndrome was described in the 1980s by Ann Smith, a genetic counsellor, and Ellen Magenis, a physician and chromosome expert. Chrissy had many of the typical features, including developmental delay, learning disability, low muscle tone and feeding difficulties in infancy, short stature, a flat facial appearance, chronic ear infections, hearing impairment, eye problems and sleep problems.

Associated behavioural problems that Chrissy shared with SMS children are: hyperactivity, head-banging, hand-biting, picking at skin, sores, nails; pulling off fingernails and toenails (she has only done this intermittently), explosive outbursts, destructive and aggressive behaviour, arm-hugging/hand-squeezing when excited (see Prisms 1992). Despite their difficult behaviours, children with SMS are, like Chrissy, very appealing and affectionate.

The geneticist requested blood tests, looking for the characteristic deletion on chromosome 17 in people with SMS. The result was normal. However, of the syndromes considered for Chrissy so far, SMS was the one most befitting Chrissy. I was disappointed about the chromosome test result and also that, once again, medical professionals felt that the outbursts were purely behavioural. No one spoke to me about the possibility of a psychiatric condition.

Chrissy's consultant suggested that resorting to screaming and self-injury when Chrissy is frustrated, anxious, cross or tired is the only way she can express or cope with these feelings. It is also possible that this could be a way of Chrissy communicating that she is in extreme pain. The consultant acknowledged that there was a more rapid escalation on these occasions, and Chrissy was not so amenable to early interventions. The staff felt that they had seen a fair spectrum of Chrissy's behaviours, and concluded them to be not epileptic but a symptom of her severe learning difficulties, and especially her small capacity for processing information.

I concluded that Chrissy's stay at The Park Hospital had been worthwhile. Although I was disappointed that the EEG recordings were not more revealing, my views about the severity of Chrissy's learning disabilities were confirmed, and we now had a behaviour management plan on dealing with Chrissy's challenging behaviour – a range of behaviour modification techniques had been implemented with varying degrees of success. Joanne Dell, the clinical psychologist at the hospital, stated that it was important to note that Chrissy learns more slowly and that there is often little improvement in the short term.

With regard to Chrissy's repetitive questioning, the strategy would now be to repeat the response once, checking for her understanding by getting her to verbalise it. If she persisted she would be told that she will be ignored if she continues. Distracting her with an alternative activity was found to be effective. The role of antecedent events in predicting and preventing screaming episodes should also be considered. Structure ought to be a consistent feature of Chrissy's environment to help her cope with what is happening around her and provide her with a sense of control. Strategies for achieving this would now include addressing her directly or from her right side to ensure that she has heard what is being said, informing her about what she is going to do, checking for her understanding and having a timetable board with pictures or symbols to facilitate structure. This would need reviewing with her throughout the day.

Chrissy needs prior warning before introducing a change in task or activity with short, concrete instructions that she should be encouraged to repeat to ensure she has understood. She is also encouraged to say 'bye-bye' to an activity to mark its termination. A positive reinforcement programme should increase desirable social behaviours; this would be achieved by giving Chrissy immediate, tangible reinforcers, such as stars and praise. A similar system would be employed at school.

Joanne Dell felt that Chrissy was functioning at a 2–2½-year-old level and that Chrissy's abilities were much more limited than appeared on superficial contact. She added that there was no evidence of autistic features in social communication and interactions. Chrissy's behaviours, including rigidity and difficulty in moving from one activity to another, were consistent with the severe degree of her learning difficulties.

I had observed how a member of staff dealt with screaming episodes. She gave Chrissy minimal interaction and attention with no access to reinforcing stimuli. This involved no eye contact, and verbal exchanges were brief with little expression. When the outburst escalated the staff member wrapped her in a towel to contain her. When Chrissy stopped, she was asked if she was ready, accompanied by gestural prompts, such as fingers on lips. Chrissy then received immediate access to adult attention.

The hospital, Chrissy's school and I drew up management guidelines for Chrissy's behaviour. St Elizabeth's School in Much Hadham, Hertfordshire, where Chrissy is now, had added to this. The guidelines varied slightly between school and home but we tried to keep them as consistent as possible. The following is an amalgamation of them all.

Chrissy Gregory – Management guidelines

Aims:

To encourage Chrissy to learn how to share adult attention with others.

To encourage Chrissy to increase her ability to work and play independently at times.

To help Chrissy gain self-control if she is in a tantrum, upset, etc.

1. Have positive expectations of Chrissy and respond to her in a clear, confident and calm way. Never show her that you are dithering!

2.   It is important for Chrissy to know and understand 'beginnings' and 'ends' of tasks/activities/conversations, etc.

3.   Try to allow Chrissy enough time to work through the 'setting up' and 'finishing' process of a task/activity/ conversation, etc. Using a timer for meals is helpful, and you can say 'Five more minutes' (indicating the timer) if Chrissy is eating slowly. This is particularly useful if she has to be somewhere at a particular time.

4.   At school Chrissy responds positively to symbols to understand the above, alongside clear speech. Symbols (such as rebus-style pictures) are also helpful at home, along with sign language.

5.   There are several brief responses that seem to reassure Chrissy when she seeks adult attention inappropriately, such as:

> 'brilliant' (if relevant)
>
> 'well done'
>
> thumbs-up sign
>
> referring Chrissy to the appropriate symbol again with minimum speech.

In this way Chrissy has been acknowledged by the adult with minimum disruption to the person or activity the adult is involved with.

6.   Sometimes Chrissy continues to repeat a question after she has understood the answer.

Say that you will answer for the last time, then that is it, no more questions. If she asks again, try saying: 'What did I say?' Chrissy will usually repeat the answer and follow it through. You can then praise her – 'brilliant' or 'well done', etc. If Chrissy gets obsessive and repetitive, do not let yourself get caught up in it. Change the subject, put music on, distract her. Sometimes Chrissy cannot be distracted from picking her fingers. Gloves are helpful with this.

7. Do not ask Chrissy open-ended questions. Always give *two* choices (she cannot cope with more). For example, if you want her to go to the toilet, try saying: 'Do you want to go on your own to the toilet, or do you want me to take you?' Never just ask: 'Do you need the toilet?' Make sure she washes her hands afterwards. All aspects of hygiene need intervention.

8. Chrissy responds to 'This first, then...' (used alongside symbols and sign language). Try to give Chrissy some kind of schedule. She needs to know where she is and where she is going to be as much as possible. If she gets agitated, give her space if that is what she needs or try music. Do not ask her if she wants music. Just put it on. You could say something like 'Sssh, you'll upset X' (another child) when she shouts. School staff use a 'shouting area', which can defuse the situation. Sometimes Chrissy feels so silly when she goes there that she will come back in.

9. Difficult situations may sometimes be defused by a smile and a joke. Chrissy can be distracted and respond well (even when she is upset or in a tantrum) to gentle, light humour, smiles, etc. It seems to reassure her that all is well.

10. Sometimes Chrissy needs removing from the situation to a quiet, distraction-free area such as the toilets at school or garden at home when:

    a) she is disrupting or upsetting others with her noise or behaviour

    b) she is hurting herself and others

    c) she seems 'stuck' in the situation and unable to move herself within it.

11. If Chrissy goes into a tantrum, try to move her to the new area as calmly and quickly as possible. Avoid eye contact, and keep communication to a minimum. If you have to intervene to stop Chrissy hurting herself or others, do not give her any feedback other than necessary restraint.

12. When Chrissy become more settled and receptive, give her immediate reinforcement by following previous guidelines for communication, giving praise for positive responses. One way of telling that she has recovered from the outburst is to ask her for a cuddle. If she is able to cuddle you without trying to squeeze the life out of you, she has recovered.

13. Chrissy tends to focus on one adult, which can be totally exhausting, and it enables her to become 'stuck' in an entrenched situation. Try swapping carers if possible. When Chrissy is out of control in the residential unit of her school, carers only spend ten minutes at a time with her. The change sometimes jolts her out of her distressed state.

14. If an outburst is particularly violent and long-lasting at school, phone the nurses and they will, if necessary, give sedation. I have sedation at home to use if necessary.

This management plan has helped Chrissy to monitor her own behaviour. She self-regulates by telling herself off or talking herself 'down'. Not every strategy works every time; but having them is reassuring, and ensures consistency between home, school and respite care. I have since been taught restraint techniques and ways of moving Chrissy with another adult's help. In-patient assessment was the best way of observing Chrissy's behaviour, and enabling consistency of care, therefore ensuring that her management plan was as concise and workable as possible.

CHAPTER 16

Making Progress

Because Chrissy was so similar to children with Smith–Magenis syndrome, I got back to Chrissy's geneticist at Great Ormond Street. He saw Chrissy again and said that the geneticists were very struck by Chrissy's behavioural phenotype, in particular her tendency to self-mutilate around her nails and skin of her finger tips. They, like the other geneticist we saw, wondered about SMS. The Great Ormond Street Hospital geneticist said that they cannot be certain yet what the sensitivity of the SMS test is, and suggested that Chrissy may well fit into that group when a better and more specific test became available. They had seen other children with the Smith–Magenis phenotype, but without the critical chromosome deletion. He felt that, with the limits of current technology, it was most unlikely that they could diagnose all those cases. He considered another syndrome – Prader–Willi – but that was later discounted. He felt that it would be useful for us to be in touch with Dr Jeremy Turk at St George's Hospital, who was interested in the behaviour problems of children with SMS. Chrissy was seen by Jeremy Turk's colleague in April 1995.

The doctor we saw felt that, although Chrissy has some of the SMS behavioural and developmental features, she did not have all characteristic physical features. She recommended that Chrissy have checks for retinal detachment, a common problem with SMS children. Chrissy had the tests, and her eyes were fine.

Despite the increasingly unlikely prospect of Chrissy being diagnosed with SMS, I read everything I could find on it. I even went to a conference, where I learned how parents and professionals managed typical SMS behaviours. I was particularly interested in theories about the prolonged outbursts (more about them in Chapter 17). I have recently picked up some tips from SMS parents, which apply to many children with learning disabilities. A couple of these are:

- If your child has no concept of time and becomes agitated when asked to complete tasks: Write a list of routine activities that you want your child to co-operate with, and draw or paste a small picture of the activity next to the word. For example: BEFORE SCHOOL 1. Get washed 2. Get dressed 3. Eat breakfast 4. Brush teeth 5. Get in the taxi or bus. This can be continued AFTER SCHOOL 1. Watch TV 2. Eat a snack 3. Go out to play. Each time your child finishes something they cross it off the list themselves. Laminating these activity sheets helps them to last longer.

- Many children with learning disabilities find it hard to differentiate between people they know well and strangers. Try the 'circle game'. Write the names of all the people your child knows on individual pieces of paper. Sit your child on the floor and arrange the pieces of paper in circles around your child. The 'cuddle' circle is closest to the child, and would include immediate family. The 'hug' circle is next, and would probably include grandparents, aunts, uncles and very close friends. The 'wave' circle comes next, and would include neighbours you do not know very well, and other people you may see regularly. The 'stranger' circle would have people like cashiers in supermarkets, or anyone else that you would consider strangers. When you have done this several times, encourage your child to do it. Other family members may also join in the game with names in their own circles.

These tips appeared in a Smith–Magenis Foundation newsletter.

A school report in the spring of 1996 was positive regarding progress in all curriculum areas, but it stressed that Chrissy's degree of participation and level of performance continued to depend upon her mood and behaviour. School staff also observed that, during Chrissy's outbursts, it was as if she experienced 'some irritation or disturbance, such as having a fit'. However, since Chrissy's hospital stay and the implementation of the behaviour management programme, the outbursts were comparatively infrequent and manageable.

Chrissy's school noted the value of a home/school diary with which we could exchange news and views about Chrissy. Another useful tactic they used was to help pupils to compile the record of achievements file, which I mentioned earlier. It included photos of school life and captions. Chrissy was proud of hers, and often asked to look through it. Throughout the day, school used symbol/word cards on a schedule (timetable) board, which helped Chrissy to gain a better understanding of what activities she would be doing and when. Often, showing Chrissy appropriate symbol cards, which she liked to hold, helped her to focus more clearly on what was being said by her teacher.

The school also noted that Chrissy tended to 'talk at' people rather than with them. She continued to self-regulate by talking about her feelings or displays of frustration in the third person. She had problems with words opposite in meaning, describing 'little' as 'big' and saying 'up' instead of 'down'. This was felt to be more a problem with language than confusion about what she was seeing.

Chrissy was making strides with reading, but she tended to read each word in isolation, showing a limited understanding of the sentence as a whole. However, she was delighted when she came across a word that she recognised from another context. Chrissy still enjoyed using computers. At school, she used 'The Oxford Reading Tree' programs, and was able to use them independently. (Chrissy is a menace with our home computers. We have an anti-virus program, but it is ineffective against 'Chrissy viruses'!)

As part of Chrissy's social education, school staff tried to prepare her for outings by explaining where they would be going, and whom she would be going with. But Chrissy's behaviour on outings remained unpredictable. Sometimes she would be sensible and take an interest in her surroundings; other times she would display disruptive behaviour, such as lying on the ground and shouting.

Often, Chrissy would come home from school with a sticker. When asked what it was for she would say, proudly: 'This is for being good in…' Pupils would be awarded stickers in the 'News and Stickers' time at the end of the day as they talked about the things they had achieved that day, and were applauded by the school. Chrissy loves communal gatherings and celebrations, especially where food, singing and dancing are involved.

Chrissy gains great pleasure from music, and moves in different ways to express rhythm. She can use simple percussion instruments to make music. Her music teacher observed that often she denied herself this pleasure because of her preoccupation with demands for attention.

Chrissy remained under review at the Oxford hospital. Her consultant wrote to Chrissy's social worker in October 1995, explaining that Chrissy's behaviour still remained extremely difficult, despite the behaviour management plan, and they were all amazed at how we had coped at home, albeit with help from local professionals. They supported my efforts to keep Chrissy living at home with me, but Chrissy's consultant wrote that I was unlikely to do so for long without further help. She asked the social worker to review the situation again to see if more help could be offered.

Meanwhile, the University of Hertfordshire contacted me about having student nurses placed with me as part of their special needs training. I had found having someone else with me helpful when dealing with Chrissy's behaviour, although I could only call on the nurses intermittently; Chrissy's consultant felt that care would be more effective if it were continuous rather than intermittent.

CHAPTER 17

Adolescence and the Importance of a Diagnosis

Chrissy's challenging behaviour escalated again. As she grew bigger she started lashing out at adults. This usually only happened in outbursts but it still sometimes caught me unawares. We had another appalling incident in our local supermarket when I had to get customers to help me carry Chrissy to my car again. At school she threw a toy in temper and accidentally knocked a teacher's tooth out.

Poor Alex was knocked down by a car in May 1996 when we were out with Chrissy. I felt guilty that I had been there, yet not prevented it. I was so preoccupied with watching Chrissy (who had no road sense) that I did not notice Alex stepping into the road without looking. She had assumed a maturity beyond her years because of Chrissy's needs, and I expected her to be safe near roads. But she had taken antihistamine medication for an allergic reaction to mosquito bites she had sustained on a recent holiday. It made her drowsy and affected her judgement. I should have taken extra care. As it was, she literally walked into the side of a passing car and bounced off it into the kerb. She had a gaping gash in her head and kept losing consciousness. It was terrifying. Luckily, we had a nurse with us at the time. She took Chrissy home while I went in the ambulance with Alex to the hospital. She recovered well, but still has a scar.

The incident highlighted how narrow my focus was when I was out with Chrissy. When crossing the road, all I worried about was her safety. Maybe it could have happened to anyone. But I cannot help thinking that I should have prevented it somehow. A split second earlier and the car would have hit Alex head on. She would have been killed.

At the end of the summer term in 1996 there was a school review about Chrissy's care. I was tearful at the review because I was beginning to believe that residential school was the only option, and I was resistant to the idea. To my relief a home care package was suggested. School wanted a full-time person in class who was available to help Chrissy and I was offered home care too.

It was like a reprieve. An extra pair of hands that would help me cope in the dreaded summer holidays. Also, in August 1996 I was booked in for a hysterectomy at West Herts Hospital. I had no idea how I would manage during the recovery period. An added factor was that Ian was offered a job in Southampton, and would be less available in the evenings because he would not be home until late each night. Then there was my back. On one occasion I put it out so completely that I could not walk, sit or do anything for about a week. I had three prolapsed discs, and had to have manipulation under general anaesthetic to help me become mobile again.

The home care would be funded jointly by the local health and education authorities and social services, and would be provided by a home carers' agency. During term time agency staff would spend 30 hours a week in school, and ten hours at home, plus four hours every second weekend. During the holidays we would have 16 hours a week care at home. Respite care was also able to make use of the carers.

A GP at my local practice would come out to administer emergency sedation by injection should Chrissy become temporarily unmanageable and violent at home, school or respite. Various methods of sedation had been used in emergencies with Chrissy. The school's doctor (Janet Hislop) suggested putting Chrissy on a low dose of haloperidol, which they had found helpful in another child with similar difficulties. It seemed to calm her down, but the side-effects were unpleasant. Procyclidine was added to counteract the shaking caused by the haloperidol. Ironically, Chrissy being sedated was something I had feared would happen if she went to residential school. Other milder sedatives had been used with varying effects. Once, after Melleril was given in an emergency that appeared to have passed, I took Chrissy swimming. She became increasingly agitated, and threw herself in the deep end of the pool. I later learnt it was a psychotic reaction to the drug.

Our contingency plans were by no means foolproof. In October 1997 Chrissy had a prolonged outburst at school. It took a teacher and two teaching assistants to move Chrissy into a 'safe' area. Also, Chrissy had wet herself, and needed to be changed. In the outburst Chrissy thrashed around, kicking, throwing and mutilating herself. She had also stripped all her clothes off, and was completely uncontrollable. Such outbursts had reached a peak again, and they were particularly protracted and unmanageable. This one went on for an hour; and all this time, her individual school management plan was being carefully followed by a number of staff members, who were all waiting to go home. Chrissy's home/school transport had to leave Chrissy at school, as they had other pupils to get home. Chrissy kept flaring up, then briefly going quiet – but could not be consoled. Eventually, she co-operated with getting dressed, then ran outside again…

Meanwhile, the school's head phoned me at home, and I subsequently phoned the surgery, after my GP had said earlier in the day at a multi-professional meeting that they would respond to this sort of emergency. However, another GP at the practice told me to call an ambulance. I telephoned the message through to the school, who called an ambulance. The ambulance crew said that they were unable to 'forcibly' remove Chrissy from school and get her on the ambulance. The ambulance staff then telephoned the GP to ask him themselves if he would come out, but were told no. So the school rang me again and I made plans to come up and try to resolve the situation. Meanwhile, the GP rang back again to say that if there were still problems after 5pm, he would come out to the school, but only if I was there. He then said that he would not sedate Chrissy at school, only at home.

I managed to leave Alex with someone, and arrived at the school to find that Chrissy had calmed down, but was still very agitated and shaky. I took her home and the ambulance crew left. Even an hour later Chrissy was still in quite a state.

The school head phoned the GP surgery again to find out what their procedures were should such a situation happen again, and was told that the GP had agreed to come to the school in an emergency situation without consulting the other GPs at the practice. I later received a phone call from the GP the head had spoken to. She told me that GPs found it 'distressing' to come out to sedate Chrissy. I asked her how they thought it made me feel.

Was I a wicked mother to sanction such an extreme method of calming Chrissy down? All I know is that the alternative was far worse. To see Chrissy suffer for hours on end, unable to come out of an outburst, was far worse than the short-lived discomfort and upset she suffered when she was sedated. I appreciate that she probably suffered long-term distress because of the way the sedation had to be given. To be held down and overpowered by adults bigger than her must have been traumatic, but what else was there?

The doctor from the practice said that the GPs did not understand Chrissy's problems because they were so complex. I told her that it was about time they acquainted themselves with Chrissy's medical needs. I wrote a letter soon after to the practice, outlining Chrissy's problems, and offered to come to a practice meeting to try to resolve things. In response, my offer was not taken up.

There had been ongoing problems with the GPs over Chrissy. When Chrissy's GP used to come out to Chrissy when she had runs of seizures, he had asked more than once: 'Who's her GP?' Another time, when on a callout because Chrissy was self-mutilating in a prolonged outburst, he asked me 'Did you do that?' when referring to her lacerated face. He said that doctors are obliged to ask questions like that when they walk into a situation like this. I could understand why a doctor would ask this question if they did not know the child's history. But he should have been well aware that Chrissy's self-harm was a major feature of her outbursts.

When I asked my GP for referrals I had been turned down. The first time was over in-patient assessment. The second time concerned taking blood for genetic tests. Our geneticist was astounded at my

GP's attitude after telephoning him to discuss the matter. I will not repeat what the eminent geneticist called him!

My GP explained his refusal by saying: 'I can't see what difference a diagnosis will make. It won't change things.'

Unfortunately, some doctors do not understand the importance of a diagnosis. At the Smith–Magenis conference, I was pleased when a doctor spoke about the importance of a diagnosis. Parents who had waited years to find out what was wrong with their child talked about the difference a diagnosis had made to their lives.

It is natural to want to know the cause of your child's disability (see Menday, Partridge and Shelley 1997). Without a clear diagnosis you can feel in limbo, trying to come to terms with what is happening and unsure about what the future holds for your child and the rest of the family. Parents often worry that their child will be deprived of appropriate services because they have no 'label'. Grief starts from the moment of diagnosis (see Greene *et al.* 1992). I felt that my grief was protracted and unfocused because I had no starting point and no reference point. You have no idea what to expect or look out for. You do not know what aspects of your child are inherent and what are unique to him or her. For instance, if Chrissy had a specific condition and I had known that Chrissy's outbursts were common in children with this condition, I would not have felt so helpless. The feeling that I was inadvertently causing them or making them worse caused me a great deal of anxiety.

Giving a name to your child's condition gives some indication of how your child may develop and helps you to explain to others what is wrong. You also feel less isolated because there are support groups for specific conditions. It is easier to find other parents experiencing similar difficulties to yours, and to get the necessary support. Talking to parents of children with Smith–Magenis syndrome was useful for me because Chrissy shared some of the perplexing behavioural characteristics. I heard theories about the prolonged bouts of distress from the conference I attended. I took them to Janet Hislop, who was very interested in them.

CHAPTER 18

Deciding to Let Go

One of the theories from the Smith–Magenis conference was that the periods of distress coupled with obsessive-compulsive behaviour could be part of a tic disorder. Chrissy had facial tics, but that theory did not fit the pattern of her outbursts. Another theory was that some behavioural and language difficulties, as characterised by autistic spectrum disorders, dyslexia and attention deficit disorder, are due to the action of an excess of certain naturally produced chemicals (opioid peptides) affecting neurological transmission. Self-harm and a high pain threshold often go hand in hand with such behaviour.

There has been lots of publicity about the link between food intolerances and autistic spectrum disorders. Reports suggest that most autistic children suffer from intestinal permeability, whereby damage to the gut wall means that it is like a sieve, allowing toxins and undigested food particles to leak into the bloodstream (e.g. Shattock *et al.* 1990). This can lead to an intolerance of gluten and casein, which, if not fully digested, takes the form of the morphine-like peptides that affect neurological transmission. In January 1998 Janet Hislop suggested we try Chrissy on a low dose of naltrexone, a drug that blocks the action of these peptides. At that time I did not quite understand the theories behind it. All I knew was that naltrexone is commonly used to help heroin addicts with withdrawal symptoms, and has been effective in some cases where children self-harm.

Janet Hislop consulted Paul Gringrass at Harper House Children's Services in Radlett. Paul had recently been looking in some detail at unusual drug regimes for teenagers with learning difficulties and behaviour problems. He had seen beneficial results with naltrexone in children with similar behaviour problems to Chrissy's. An added benefit of naltrexone is that side-effects are thought to be minor and only occur in about 10 per cent of individuals.

I learnt about dietary intervention theories when I read an article in *You* magazine entitled 'Thank you for saving my son from autism'. The article mentioned Paul Shattock, who works at the Autism Research Unit at the University of Sunderland. Testing the urine of susceptible children was a good indicator of whether excluding casein and gluten would be beneficial. I sent a sample of Chrissy's urine to Paul Shattock.

The test results indicated that Chrissy would benefit from excluding gluten and casein. The exclusion of gluten and casein under Great Ormond Street's few-foods diet did not yield any remarkable changes in Chrissy's behaviour, but effects can take a while to become noticeable. However, Chrissy already limits her own diet to such an extent (often children who are affected by these foods become addicted to them, like an addict craves drugs) that we decided, after speaking to medical professionals involved in her care, to leave it until we run out of other options. After all, the use of naltrexone should have a similar effect to excluding casein and gluten.

Chrissy's outbursts became shorter with less self-harm for a while after the introduction of naltrexone. When Chrissy's medical team gradually withdrew naltrexone nearly two years later to see if it really was having any beneficial effects, her self-harm escalated dramatically. She focused on the fingers of one hand, bending them back and picking them until they bled. This did not happen in an outburst, just during the course of the day. The staff put gardening gloves on her in an attempt to stop her mutilating her hands. When Chrissy is going through a picking phase it is difficult to distract her and get her to do anything else. We can now safely say that naltrexone has been successful with Chrissy.

Three months into Chrissy's new drug regime we noticed short episodes where Chrissy's left foot dragged and her speech was slurred. But she immediately recovered and I wondered whether she was just mucking about. A month later, in April 1998, she showed a strange reaction after the GP gave her an emergency haloperidol injection. Chrissy had been screaming non-stop for over an hour, and the outburst was increasing in intensity as it went on. After the injection Chrissy calmed down, then her speech became slurred and her left foot dragged, as before. This time, however, her eyes rolled, and her mouth and face drooped. This lasted for half an hour. It looked like a dystonic reaction – she became extremely vacant. In hospital Chrissy once had a dystonic reaction to a drug they gave her. I found out later by chance, when looking up something else on the internet, that such a reaction was known as 'Todd's paralysis'. It is normally part of a partial seizure. On our doctor's advice we gave Chrissy procyclidine, which aborted the reaction.

Once again, Chrissy's behaviour deteriorated. In extreme outbursts Chrissy ate her own faeces and lashed out at adults. The effectiveness of haloperidol was wearing off and it was causing more problems than it solved. We had tried every available treatment, but nothing worked long-term. I contacted the local surgery again.

The GPs, in a written response, made it clear that they would only visit me at home. They would not be prepared to go to school, respite or any other public place. They made my local casualty department aware of Chrissy's problems by providing me with a letter to keep with me in public places. Thus, if Chrissy had to go to casualty by ambulance the letter would indicate to doctors what emergency medication to give her. The GP also wrote that all the practice doctors were now more aware of Chrissy and her history. If the measures they suggested did not work they offered to meet with me to discuss the next range of options. I informed them that the measures they suggested were not working and for the first time, my GP came along to a review meeting and asked sympathetic questions about Chrissy. I spent the meeting either crouched by a chair or standing up. My back was giving out under the repeated strain of lifting, moving and restraining Chrissy.

I had Chrissy's siblings and Ian to consider. As Chrissy got bigger Alex got even more frightened when Chrissy was uncontrollable.

Poor Ian often came home from work to find Alex and me crying, property broken, and Chrissy covered in self-inflicted injuries. Was it fair on him?

As the school half-term holiday in May 1998 drew nearer, things got worse. Calling GPs out was impractical most of the time because they had other patients to see and often could not come for an hour or so. Even with two of us (myself and a carer), property was wrecked and Chrissy was unmanageable. The home care agency was unhappy about its carers being exposed to situations where they could get hurt. The more aware Chrissy became of her increasing physical power, the more she used it to hurt adult carers. I felt terribly sad about this, because she was basically a gentle child. School staff were struggling too, despite the extra helper. It took three people to move Chrissy when she was uncontrollable. Something had to give.

Local health and care professionals had put in all the community-based services that they could to help us cope at home. The next step for Chrissy was residential school and I knew the time had come for us to decide whether to let her go. Even though Chrissy was a teenager, nearing the time that non-disabled children start breaking away, it is still hard. Remember that, developmentally, many of these teenagers are like toddlers, and it is heart-wrenching to part with a child who is that dependent on you. I knew I would miss Chrissy dreadfully, and wondered how she would cope.

Would she forget who we were? Conversely, how would I feel if she clung to me when I left her there after visits home? What if we gradually filled the gap she had left in our lives, and visited her less and less often? Would they keep her clean and nicely dressed? Would they sedate her every time she got agitated, without waiting to see if the outburst would abate without intervention? But maybe I was denying Chrissy a better life. Perhaps she would thrive in a more structured environment.

We had a school review and I agreed to look at a termly boarding school, St Elizabeth's in Much Hadham, Hertfordshire. The school provides a residential setting for pupils with epilepsy and learning difficulties. It has small teaching groups and a multidisciplinary team of specialist teachers, an onsite speech and language therapist, a phsyiotherapist, educational psychologist and full-time medical team. Each child has regular multidisciplinary assessments. Medical specialists visit the children at the school – much easier than the hikes up to Great Ormond Street for a five-minute appointment.

I went to see the school in May 1998 and had a good feeling about it. I had been uneasy about the school's Christian ethos: nuns play an active part in the running of St Elizabeth's. But I had no need to worry about my own non-beliefs. Many other parents are non-believers too, and the children can only benefit from being in a Christian environment. The sense of peace and the staff's dedication to the children's well-being is palpable at St Elizabeth's. The serenity of their surroundings surely helps them to cope with the inner turmoil caused by their epilepsy and learning disabilities. The children I saw looked happy and cared for.

From a medical point of view, it would be possible to monitor Chrissy's changeable condition more intensively there, and perhaps stabilise it. It would also give a better opportunity for new treatments to be tried out under medical supervision. It would be a great relief to share Chrissy's ongoing medical needs with qualified staff. She could come home at weekends and during school holidays. I was assured that Janet Hislop would provide medical backup in emergencies and I would still have agency carers at home. However, Chrissy would not be able to start until after the summer holidays. If there was any lingering doubt about deciding to let Chrissy go, events over the next few months were to dispel them!

Things came to a head again over the school holidays in May 1998. One day Chrissy was severely distressed for such a long period that I called an ambulance, and went to casualty with her, asking them to admit her. Chrissy was given a mattress on the floor of a room in the ward. I looked at her, naked, screaming and covered in cuts and bruises, and told stunned nursing staff: 'I'm leaving her here until someone does something about these outbursts.'

It was one of the hardest things I have ever done. Ian backed me completely.

'The only way we'll get anything effective done is to let other people deal with Chrissy in this state,' he insisted when my resolve weakened.

The sister on the children's ward took one look at Chrissy and announced: 'That's not learning disabilities; that's psychosis.'

Chrissy stayed on the ward for two weeks until her condition was stabilised. Her drug regime was completely overhauled. I was no longer prepared to deal with these severe outburts at home. After that first night away from her I came and spent time with her in hospital. I did not want to take over her care because I needed staff to report back on how her behaviour was.

Janet Hislop supervised dramatic medication changes with the help of the hospital consultants. In hospital Chrissy's condition veered from being out of control to a 'frozen' state where she did not want to move, get dressed or do anything that involved change. She became constipated and barely ate. Hospital staff tried to sedate Chrissy only when absolutely necessary, yet there were still occasions where they had to hold her down and inject paraldehyde.

A psychiatrist came to see Chrissy in hospital. He noted that she seemed anxious and obsessive, picking constantly at her nails and flapping her hands. He had an interesting view on Chrissy's mental state: he thought she was suffering from a mental illness – cyclic depression. At first, I was sceptical, but the psychiatrist said that depression in learning disabled people does not always manifest itself in the same way as it does in people without learning disabilities. The psychiatric dimension is often neglected in people with learning disabilities, particularly in children and adolescents (Marcheschi, Masi and Pfanner 1998). All the types of mental disorders can be observed in these people, with a prevalence estimated to be at least three or four times higher than the general population (Graham, Rutter and Yule 1970).

People with learning disabilities can experience the full range of emotional disorders (Dosen and Gielen 1993; Hurley and Sovner 1983). The prevalence of depressive disorders is unclear because cognitive impairment can mask the emotional disturbance (the so-called 'diagnostic overshadowing') (Reiss 1990). The more severe the learning disability, the harder it is to diagnose depressive disorders because clinical features are less defined.

Children and adults with learning disabilities are considered particularly vulnerable to depression (Miller and Reynolds 1985). Some of the diagnostic tools developed for normal IQ subjects are then used to evaluate people with learning disabilities. It is important to ask carers to report their observations. Crying and irritability are commonly observed by respondents, as are a specifically depressed mood, psychomotor agitation and loss of energy and interest. Functional symptoms (such as disturbed sleep, appetite loss, etc.) are less frequent than emotional and psychomotor symptoms.

I was interested to note in the clinical study conducted by Marcheschi *et al.* (1998) that psychomotor symptoms are often mixed; lassitude and loss of energy can co-exist with episodic psychomotor agitation. This was exactly how Chrissy behaved at her worst. Perhaps what I called her 'frozen states' were just complete lassitude. Chrissy *did* suffer from the less common functional symptoms: she lost her appetite and slept excessively in these states. The outbursts could definitely be described as an extreme form of 'episodic psychomotor agitation'!

I also wondered about the 'anger turned inwards' view of depression. Chrissy often turned her anger against herself. Could a depressive disorder be the cause?

One of the nurses from the University of Hertfordshire had once, perceptively, asked me if anyone had considered the possibility of a dual diagnosis of learning disabilities and mental illness. No one other than this psychiatrist had mentioned the possibility to me. Why? I became aware that mental illness is very much under-diagnosed in both non-disabled children and people with learning disabilities.

The psychiatrist at the hospital wanted to try Chrissy on Prozac, and although it was not licensed for children under 18, Chrissy was prescribed it. Janet Hislop decided to alter Chrissy's new medication regime gradually to observe its effects. She wondered whether Epilim was worsening Chrissy's behaviour, and started the process of reducing it whilst simultaneously introducing lamotrigine, another anticonvulsant. Chrissy developed a rash, so lamotrigine was withdrawn. She was put back on Epilim, which has remained effective for the seizures. The dose has needed fine-tuning regularly as Chrissy's weight fluctuates and her seizure frequency changes.

Haloperidol, in my view an unpleasant drug with too many side-effects, was completely withdrawn, both as regular and emergency treatment. I believe that haloperidol had contributed to Chrissy's psychotic state. Naltrexone was reduced because it was found to be more effective in smaller doses. The stimulant dextroamphetamine was tried because doctors felt that some of Chrissy's behaviour may be compulsive and part of an attention deficit disorder. Doctors also felt that it might benefit Chrissy's seizures. For once, Chrissy reacted the same way as most of us would – she was as high as a kite and could not sleep! Dextroamphetamine was withdrawn.

Intramuscular paraldehyde was used successfully to curtail extreme outbursts. Both intramuscular and rectal paraldehyde were considered too difficult to administer at home for outbursts. Chrissy would need to be restrained while it was being given. The nurses showed me how to give chlorpromazine injections as an emergency treatment at home.

Chrissy's condition was much improved on her new regime, which has continued to this day. The only changes are the addition of rectal paraldehyde, if needed, in runs of seizures, alterations in the Epilim dose and chlorpromazine tablets for extreme outbursts.

Chrissy lost weight on Prozac but looked much better for it, and was able to wear normal clothes. No wonder they call Prozac 'The Sunshine Drug'. Chrissy became much happier and her moods more stable. The new regime did not completely eliminate the outbursts, but they were generally shorter with less self-harm and no aggression to others. To see Chrissy calm without being in a stupor was wonderful. Her quality of life improved considerably after that hospital stay.

I thank Janet Hislop for effecting those necessary changes. If only all doctors were like her! She listened when I described my experiences with Chrissy, and was open-minded about my suggestions. She was brave enough to try radical new treatments. She was prepared to spend time researching the theories I mentioned, and she consulted other medical professionals who had experience in unusual drug regimes in children with challenging behaviour.

I wondered anew whether I had made the right decision about residential school. Now Chrissy's behaviour was more stable perhaps we could all cope better. But there are no miracle cures with challenging behaviour. She still had her moments!

In August 1999 Chrissy had an EEG at Great Ormond Street Hospital. Afterwards a carer, Alex and I went with Chrissy to the canteen. Chrissy became obsessed with the idea of having chocolate, and refused to budge from the chocolate vending machine. As part of her behavioural management programme she had to eat some of what was put in front of her first. I told her that she had to eat her sandwich, then she could have chocolate. She went on and on, working herself up into a state. As I tried to remove her to take her home a woman offered Chrissy's carer 50 pence to get Chrissy some chocolate. The carer patiently explained the situation. I got wind of what was happening, told the woman Chrissy was on a behaviour and eating programme, thanked her, then left.

We had to carry Chrissy out between us and when we got outside Alex said: 'That lady said horrible things in there about you, mummy. She said you're not fit to be a parent, and if Chrissy wants chocolate she should have chocolate.'

If I had not been struggling to hold Chrissy I would have gone back into the hospital and given the woman a piece of my mind.

On another occasion I took Chrissy and Alex to the local video-hire store, and Chrissy became agitated for no apparent reason. I am still suspicious about the hypnotic effect the store's flashing lights might have on her, even though it is illegal to have lights flashing at a certain frequency known to affect those suffering from photo-sensitive epilepsy. I tried at first to distract Chrissy and get her into the car as quickly as possible. But she had gone out of control too quickly for early intervention to work. I sat next to her on the floor, hoping the outburst would be short-lived. A long queue was forming at the counter, and we were the side-show!

Chrissy sank deeper and deeper into her outburst, and I knew we would be there for a long time. Alex was getting distressed and I felt the old, familiar feelings of helplessness wash over me. I sent Alex off to ask someone for help in getting Chrissy to my car. A well-built youth walked uneasily over to us, and I repeated my request. He helped me to carry Chrissy outside the store, and reluctantly agreed to stay with Chrissy, with Alex's help, while I brought the car right up to the kerb (which only took a minute). We bundled Chrissy awkwardly into the car. And she kicked upwards, shattering my windscreen. Her nose had started bleeding in the struggle too. I just thanked the youth, and drove home.

Ian was stunned when we arrived home, bloody and tearful, with my shattered windscreen. We had only gone to hire a video! As Alex flung herself into Ian's arms, beside herself with anguish, and as I poured myself a stiff drink, my feelings about residential school crystallised. We had to give it a go. I was reassured by professionals involved in our decision that, at any stage, we could change our minds and have Chrissy back home if things did not work out. I also hoped, probably in vain, that Chrissy's behaviour (particularly the outbursts) might be stabilised enough to have her home permanently again.

Chrissy started at St Elizabeth's School in September 1998 as a weekly boarder. It is completely geared up for her complex needs in a way we could not hope to equal at home. We choose to have her home most weekends, and she stays with us during the school holidays. It was like a bereavement at first. I kept looking at Chrissy's empty room and bursting into tears. I was suffering prematurely from the 'empty nest syndrome'. But each time I let Chrissy go a little – the first night she spent in respite care, the first MENCAP holiday she went on, then residential school – I have looked back and recognised that I made the right decision for her – and our family.

As another mum told me when her child started weekly boarding school: 'My daughter was thriving there. But I wasn't sure I'd made the right decision, until the school's headmistress said that letting her go was the most loving thing I could ever do for her.'

I acknowledge that residential school is not necessarily the best choice for every family, but it was for ours. I know of mothers with disabled children who will not let go. They think that putting their child in a home is giving up on them. I also know mums whose disabled children rule the roost. To me, that means you are not coping with your child.

A carer told me about a child she looked after who ran amok in his home. His three siblings suffered; his mum and dad became ill. His parents felt guilty even putting him in respite care. When his dad brought him along, the child kept biting him. His dad shrugged his shoulders and said: 'What can I do? He can't help it.'

However, the carers were not prepared to put up with being bitten. And the father's passive acceptance of his child's unacceptable behaviour made their job harder.

'These behaviours may be the norm at home,' the carer said, 'but one day your child won't have you around and you need to prepare them for that. What's cute in a toddler is not cute in an adult, with or without learning disabilities. No one appreciates an overgrown baby who bites and cannot do anything for itself. The child was capable of far more. But they held him back by treating him like a baby.'

When she told me this story Chrissy was screaming and self-harming. I just got on with my ironing, keeping an eye on any breakable household possessions as I did so.

'You're in control,' the carer said.

'I haven't always been,' I admitted.

It is only by having adequate help that I have been able to regain that control. My back problems meant I was unable to lift Chrissy at all by then, which made me feel particularly vulnerable and powerless when dealing alone with an outburst. On one occasion I had insisted Chrissy help clear up the mess she had made during a deliberately destructive act (once she had calmed down). I had already received a smack in the face when I got too close. The carer's observations made me realise how far we had come already.

I had wondered how I would fill the empty hours. But I soon found my time taken up with the rest of my family and a new career in freelance journalism. My jewellery business had gone down the pan just over two years before because the company went bankrupt. I used my experiences with Chrissy as a launch pad into journalism.

Many of my features have been about issues surrounding children with behaviour problems. Though I write about other issues too, some serious, others light-hearted, mainly for women's magazines.

Now I know how other families live. I do not have the unease every morning of wondering what mood Chrissy will wake up in; I don't spend the day with my stomach in knots because she might have an outburst after school. I look forward to her coming home at weekends, and we all have more time and patience with her then. The downside of having a child with challenging behaviour at residential school is, for me, more than outweighed by the benefits.

CHAPTER 19

Residential School – Making a Difference

Chrissy settled in well at St Elizabeth's. The transition period from her previous school was smoothed by using similar symbols and structure, such as the individual behaviour management plan. We had already been there on a visit with Chrissy, and had showed her around. We were encouraged to provide photos of Chrissy's 'other life' so that she had reference points about people she knew and things that she had done at home.

During the first two weekends at home Chrissy watched videos of her previous class at school. She was initially confused about which school she was going to on the Monday. I talked it through with her, using names she knew and the information brochure from St Elizabeth's (which contains photos of the school). One thing that helped her to differentiate between schools was that a taxi picked her up, rather than a bus. She went off to her new school happily enough when Monday mornings came.

Chrissy's story has now reached the present. All my fears about residential school have melted away. Chrissy does not get upset when she leaves us at the start of the week; yet she is always pleased to see us when she comes home. Her behaviour is less volatile; yet she remains alert, something that I did not think was possible. Taking her out in public can still be difficult, but is much improved. We are planning a short holiday to Disneyland in Paris next year, and we will see how Chrissy copes with a view to taking her on more holidays in future.

Chrissy has started interacting beautifully with her peers. She has not built a special relationship with a particular child, but they all like her. It looks like she has reached another developmental stage. She teases other children light-heartedly, and watches them playing. She seems to learn from them. Though she is still small she thinks she is much smaller than her actual size – we took her to the park recently, where she insisted on going in the baby swings (she just about fits in).

'Hello, boy!' she said, cheerfully, to the child in the next swing. 'I copy you.'

Then Chrissy went on the roundabout. A girl of about 11 went to lift a toddler off it. Chrissy noticed what was happening and put her arms up. The bemused girl heaved her off too!

I laughed about this incident later with mum, who said: 'That's marvellous news. I remember when Chrissy used to look so isolated and in her own world at times.'

Staff at St Elizabeth's are not fazed by Chrissy's behaviour. Many other pupils have outbursts and challenging behaviour, though the outbursts are not as long as Chrissy's. It is apparent that staff are fond of Chrissy, and give her lots of hugs and affection. They talk about her with warmth and amusement, which is reassuring. I was surprised at how severe Chrissy's epilepsy was regarded at St Elizabeth's. The school's targets were to teach Chrissy better interaction with the other pupils, to help her develop more understanding of what is being said to her, to make her more independent in carrying out tasks, and to modify her behavioural outbursts. Chrissy still has a one-to-one worker at school. At her 'home unit' at school there are more behaviour problems, as there are at home with us, because the structure is not so easy to maintain. There is also a lower ratio of staff to children.

Her blood levels are regularly checked and sometimes her medication is adapted. Even subtle increases and decreases in one drug can affect her. Epilim has recently been reduced slightly because Chrissy was losing too much weight, and had gone off her food. She then had a nasty seizure, so it was upped again slightly. I could not equal this degree of monitoring at home.

Despite ambulatory monitoring having indicated that Chrissy's vacant spells were not epileptic absences, St Elizabeth's staff feel that she does have absences, and have recorded up to 20 in one day. When Chrissy recovers she immediately begins to say one of her familiar phrases or comments to let herself know that she has come back to reality. School staff feel that many of her anxieties about what she is doing tie in closely to the absences and could be linked to some of her behavioural patterns.

Both simple and complex partial seizures have been observed by staff. Although it is felt unlikely at St Elizabeth's that any of Chrissy's behaviour problems are seizures, the staff have written that they have 'no doubt that her severe epilepsy has a significant effect on her behaviour'. EEGs still do not indicate the severity of Chrissy's epilepsy, though they show her potential for it. It could be that her epilepsy originates from a deeper source than the electrodes can record. Or maybe, what appear to be absences are some other form of dissociation from what is going on around her. Chrissy has been given rectal paraldehyde only once at St Elizabeth's to terminate seizures, and we have used it successfully at home on one occasion. The major seizures always occur at night now.

Chrissy's behaviour still causes concern, though short outbursts have decreased. They occur mainly when she is overexcited about an event, when she is unsure about a task, when she has been asked to complete a task that she finds too difficult, or when she is asked to wait longer than she can bear for her turn in an activity. Chrissy remains easily distracted, and needs regular refocusing by adults. She is still demanding of adult attention, but more aware of how her screaming upsets other pupils. School staff feel that they can contain 80 per cent of Chrissy's outbursts with consistent handling by familiar staff. When she is out of control the staff follow the agreed school policy of 'TEAM-TEACH' methods where strategies are used to reinforce positive behaviour and safely de-escalate crisis situations. This involves star charts, distraction tactics, escorting, holding and, when needed, restraining.

Staff understand that Chrissy's development is hindered by outbursts and stressful moments. They appreciate her needs to have sequences to events, to keep her on track and reduce stress levels. To enable her to understand 'beginnings' and 'ends' Chrissy needs to be fully involved and aware of events. To help her achieve this she has her timetable and social activities clearly sequenced with symbols. She puts together her timetable for specified time periods in the day, using symbols. She has with her at each activity a symbol appropriate to the task involved at that particular time.

Chrissy still has outbursts lasting up to two hours that have proved very distressing to staff, but these are usually on the home unit at St Elizabeth's where there is a less structured environment. Once or twice, nursing staff have been called to the home unit to administer sedation during prolonged outbursts, but they were unsuccessful in getting the tablet into Chrissy's mouth.

On the home unit, she enjoys playing on the computer, watching videos and listening to music. She also enjoys books and one-to-one activities with an adult. There are large tricycles that Chrissy can ride around the grounds. She often goes on outings to McDonald's and other places in the local community. However, her behaviour can swing dramatically from being co-operative, calm and chatty, to screaming, demanding, repetitive questioning and self-harm. Generally, this has diminished recently, but the home unit staff commented that, at times, you could almost feel there was a switch that changes Chrissy's behaviour.

Sometimes whispering and a calm approach works. Chrissy's teacher, Pauline Mullins, has devised a new method of dealing with Chrissy's more destructive behaviours. If Chrissy shouts and makes a noise to gain attention, school staff deal with it in the ways mentioned previously – no reinforcing stimuli. If, however, Chrissy is throwing things and hurting herself, two members of staff 'sandwich' her between them on chairs. If Chrissy is on the floor, a third member of staff may need to help lift Chrissy on to the chair. One member of staff sits behind Chrissy, holding her arms across her chest in a recognised method of restraint. She tells Chrissy firmly: 'You're tense, calm down', etc. The other member of staff sits in front of Chrissy, on the floor, to make Chrissy feel less intimidated. She then 'showers' Chrissy with positive, gentle words, body language and gestures, while stroking Chrissy's hands. Apparently, this method is reducing the duration of the outbursts. I wondered whether it might reinforce Chrissy's 'bad behaviour'. But, as Pauline Mullins pointed out, these particular behaviours are as a result of inner turmoil, negative feelings that Chrissy cannot bear and wants to stop, not 'naughtiness'.

I have tried doing something similar at home when Chrissy gets agitated. I 'shower' her with positive language to distract her. This method makes sense for a child with a depressive illness. Ignoring her and avoiding eye contact will, if she is already feeling terrible about herself, only make things worse. The important thing is to different-iate between those behaviours that are due to overwhelming feelings of anxiety and sadness, and those that are attention seeking and within Chrissy's control.

Behaviour management programmes should evolve over a period of time and be tailored to the individual's needs. The school staff and I are always looking at new ways of managing Chrissy's behaviour. I then add any successful techniques to Chrissy's behaviour manage-ment programme, which I give to home carers when they come in during the school holidays.

There have been less successful attempts at behaviour manage-ment. One idea was to reinforce good behaviour with star charts, using Coco Pops, a breakfast cereal, as a reward. But Chrissy soon became obsessive about Coco Pops, and did not understand the reason why she was reeiving them. So, after further rewards also proved unsuccessful, the plan was discontinued. There are times when Chrissy responds to behavioural management programmes like this. But there are others when Chrissy is unreceptive to any form of behavioural intervention.

Chrissy receives far more speech therapy than she ever did living at home. She is seen twice weekly, and thoroughly enjoys her sessions, especially body awareness. The speech and language therapist agrees with previous ones that the clarity and fluency of Chrissy's speech is deceptive, leading to higher expectations being made of her than she could meet. The speech therapists told me that they looked forward to the days when they have Chrissy because she is so funny and entertaining. Their comments made me glow with pride.

I realised how much Alex and Jamie had missed out because of the limitations imposed by Chrissy's behaviour. With Chrissy away at residential school both the other children can bring friends home now. It used to disrupt Chrissy's routine so much that it became impossible when she was around. Alex does all the things that ten-year-olds do, going to Guides, gym and learning the piano. I can run her about after school, whereas when Chrissy was at home I was often dealing with some crisis or other.

Jamie stays regularly, sometimes bringing his friends. I subjugated his needs out of necessity for Chrissy's, and now I can address them far more. We often discuss Jamie's emotions and try to make sense of them. He told me tearfully, soon after Chrissy went away to school, that he wished he could start his life afresh. He felt so much had gone wrong for him. Jamie's loyalties are still split, but he admits that with his father he has the freedom and lack of boundaries that he has become used to.

I sometimes felt very angry with Tony, and he with me. I felt that he was not giving Jamie's needs the priority they deserved. And he said I undermined him at every turn. But on the whole our communications about the children have improved. We are now getting family counselling from NCH Action for Children.

Jamie's disclosures, both in private and in front of the NCH worker, have been immensely painful. I went through a phase of grieving for the part of his childhood we both lost. I dwelled on 'if onlys': if only the children's birth order had been different, the children could have all stayed together; if only I could have Jamie as a baby again now, how different things would be. Sometimes, when I would see a little boy trustingly folding his chubby hand in his mother's as he bounced along by her side, I would feel bereft. That part of our relationship was shattered when Jamie went to live with his father.

Jamie remains adamant about staying with his dad despite ongoing problems there. I have had to accept that, and I no longer take it personally. Our relationship, after a great deal of work, is much closer than I ever dreamed it would be. That thought warms me through the bad times.

CHAPTER 20

Making Sense of the Past
and Looking to the Future

When Chrissy was nearly 15 we needed to prepare for her future. In March 1999 I was invited to a meeting to discuss a transition plan. The transition plan is the start of a process of careers guidance and action planning which will continue until Chrissy leaves school. Aims discussed at the meeting were to improve Chrissy's communication skills, her ability to understand events and what is being said to her, and her behaviour, so that she could enjoy life more and be as independent as possible. Additional aims I have are for her to be more a part of the family when it comes to outings and holidays. Sending her to residential school has made this more possible.

We rarely see the really prolonged outbursts anymore, but just a tiny increase or decrease in one of her drugs can upset the balance. The use of antibiotics for a gum infection worsened Chrissy's behaviour considerably, and emphasised the need for continued vigilance to keep the right balance of medication.

In November 1999 staff at St Elizabeth's informed me that she had begun another cycle of agitated behaviour without any apparent reason after a long calm period. The unprovoked outbursts inexplicably clouded her life again despite all the interventions and medication. Luckily, they were short-lived. One particularly bad one occurred after a school disco, which reinforces my rather shaky theories about links between Chrissy and flashing lights. Maybe the outbursts will continue throughout her life and we will never completely know the cause of them. But they are just a small part of the wonderful whole, and something I will have to accept and deal with as and when they occur.

We realised how far we'd come when I took Chrissy to a Millennium party organised by Mencap in January 2000. Chrissy was delightful – she joined in with the other children and bounded up to many of her old friends from her last school. I really felt that she had matured into a confident young lady and was no longer so toddler-like and needy in her social behaviour. Everyone remarked on how well she looked too. She's slimmed down (Prozac suppresses her appetite) and looks much happier. Many parents and helpers commented on how much she'd improved. One mum said, flatteringly: 'She looks lovely and slim. She's more like you now – it's as if that's how she's supposed to look.'

We took her to Disneyland, Paris, in February 2000. It was a resounding success. She had a fantastic time, though she got tired and understandably irritable towards the end of our 4-day stay and we had to hire a wheelchair. It was all the more magical for us being there with her and seeing her reactions to everything.

She shows more curiosity about her surroundings and is able to monitor her own behaviour better as her understanding about what is going on increases.

If current progress at St Elizabeth's is maintained, Chrissy will continue into the student department, where she will stay until she is 19. Her needs during that time are likely to remain the same as they are now. Beyond 19, St Elizabeth's Home may be suitable. We have been to see it, and were impressed by the facilities and care offered. Chrissy would continue to have an organised daily curriculum, with varied activities. She would also receive continuity of care within a new, yet familiar, environment.

Bringing up a child like Chrissy has been the toughest challenge I have ever faced. I was treated like an over-anxious mother when I first expressed concerns about Chrissy's development. When she showed signs of challenging behaviour, medical professionals had no more idea than I did about what was going on. Parents will continue to face delays in accessing appropriate services for challenging behaviour unless all health and care professionals become aware of the information and services available.

For so many years Chrissy's essence glimmered tantalisingly through the fog of her challenging behaviour. I ran myself ragged trying to reach it, but it remained beyond my grasp. Chrissy's potential has burgeoned and she has a better quality of life than I ever dared hoped for now her needs are being identified and addressed.

Maturity has played its part. One medical professional told me that adolescence is a watershed: Chrissy's behaviour would either deteriorate or improve. But I attribute the improvements in her behaviour mainly to a combination of the right medication and the ongoing, consistent behavioural interventions. We can never be complacent with Chrissy. Because she has not yet started her periods, we do not know how or if they will affect her behaviour.

Because I had been so absorbed in dealing with the processes surrounding being the mother of a child with challenging behaviour, I never allowed myself the space to deal with everything that has happened. Now that the dust has settled, I am struggling to overcome my feelings of failure and inadequacy. I lost all my confidence as a mother. Living with the consequences of having a child with severe learning disabilities and challenging behaviour is a rickety bridge I am still crossing. But wallowing in regrets about the past is futile. We have to move on with our lives.

We have not got a conventional family, but then Chrissy is not a conventional child. The way things are now works for us.

I no longer grieve for the 'perfect' child I should have had, because without her disability she would not be Chrissy. It is only by standing back and letting go a little that I have been able to accept and love her for who she is. I like to think that, if Chrissy could express her views, she would thank us for letting her go away to school. I believe that the good times are here to stay; Chrissy has finally found contentment and serenity.

Part 3

Therapy, Practical Help and Support

CHAPTER 21

Treatment Approaches

The evidence that positive behavioural intervention programmes reduce the frequency and severity of challenging behaviour is compelling. Many only evolve successfully when they are practised and adapted over a long period of time.

There is some evidence that medication is effective for specific indications. Other treatments may work for individual children but there is less scientific evidence regarding their efficacy. It is important that treatment approaches are rigorously monitored and reviewed, and tailored to the needs of the individual child and family.

It is important that services do not contribute to parents feeling 'blamed' for their child's challenging behaviour, and families should be involved in treatment decisions. Any treatment should be based on one or more hypotheses regarding the causes and functions of the behaviour. Treatment can then be directed at testing out these possible explanations (Wertheimer 1997).

Alternative therapies

Often parents turn to treatments, such as aromatherapy massage, reflexology, homeopathy, acupuncture, and cranial osteopathy, either when conventional medicine has not helped their child, or to complement orthodox treatments. Alternative therapies may enable parents to feel that they are taking some responsibility for their child's welfare, and some parents claim that they help the child. It is worth discussing more 'fringe treatments' with a medical professional treating your child.

Supplementary therapies

Light therapy

Some parents of Smith–Magenis children have found light therapy helpful after noticing that their child's behaviour improved on sunny days. They put a light box near the child for twenty minutes when he or she is eating breakfast.

Creative therapies

Music, art and drama therapies can help socially withdrawn children establish a relationship with an adult. The child may derive great pleasure from such therapies, and they can be a way of helping a child express itself.

Medication

Treatment with psychotropic drugs should not be used in isolation, and needs to be part of a more comprehensive treatment programme. The medication chosen needs to be targeted at specific symptoms for which there is evidence supporting its efficacy. Target symptoms need to be monitored and show improvement before continuing the use of medication. If target symptoms have been reduced or absent for a predetermined period, then an attempt should be made to reduce the dose. Proper withdrawal regimes should be planned if the medication is discontinued. Any medication prescribed should be considered in a carefully monitored therapeutic trial because responses in children with challenging behaviour can be varied. Some parents of children with Smith–Magenis syndrome have found certain medications useful; others have found that their child's behaviour is better without any. Melatonin has proved effective for some Smith–Magenis children with sleep disorders, and allowed them to sleep through the night. Preventing the child from becoming over-stimulated and over-tired can be the key to avoiding the worst full-scale, self-abusive outbursts. Beta-blockers have also been used to modify behaviour in some Smith–Magenis children. It has produced varying results and some parents have been unhappy about its side-effects.

Changing the child's environment

Ideas about this are detailed in the next chapter (p.169). Certainly, making such changes can lessen the risks to the child. For some children, particularly those with autistic spectrum disorders, a predictable environment with minimal distractions is necessary. Some children with severe challenging behaviour need to be in an environment that others would find abnormal. If this is necessary, the aim should be for the child to have access to as normal an environment as possible and unnecessary restrictions should be avoided.

Behavioural approaches

Behavioural approaches seek to eliminate or minimise specific problem behaviours. They can also be used to understand the functions of a behaviour in a particular child; that is, the settings, consequences and triggers that make a particular behaviour more likely to occur. Functional behavioural analysis and a behavioural approach may be used to manipulate the environment or to identify new skills a child needs, as well as working directly on the challenging behaviour.

Prior to intervention, functional assessment should be used to identify the purpose of the challenging behaviour in the particular child. Aims should be to introduce new skills, not simply to reduce the challenging behaviour. Intervention involves changing social systems, such as schools and the ways families interact, rather than just changing the person with the challenging behaviour. The ultimate goal of intervention is to improve people's quality of life.

It needs to be borne in mind that children behave differently in different settings. It is therefore preferable to carry out the interventions at home and at school. The professional can then advise and support those in daily contact with the child. This also means that the behaviours will be responded to consistently. Consistent responses from other people are important if the child is to benefit from the treatment, and good communication is necessary between all those involved with the child. For some children, there may need to be such a degree of consistency that it can only be achieved in a specialist residential school.

Achieving and sustaining behavioural change can be difficult and behavioural approaches may need to be used for many years.

Dietary treatment

I have touched on dietary treatments in previous chapters. There has been so much interest in diet therapies for behaviour problems that most people have heard of them (for an overview, see Hemsley and Taylor 1990). Most people are also quite confused by the amount of pseudoscience and conflicting dogmatic pronouncements. The public at large has, on the whole, been more enthusiastic about the treatment than scientists. After all it is common experience that what you eat affects the way you feel and even act.

There is no scientific agreement on whether diet treatments have any value, or whether they are safe. Like other new treatments, when diet treatments are introduced they must be compared with other treatments in controlled clinical trials, and not given routinely until the evidence is clear. Most scientific trials of diet treatments have been carried out on 'hyperactive' children. In autistic children, there is no evidence that diet is causative, and diet is not a cure. But hyperactive behaviour is a common feature in autism, and anything that can help is useful.

Two dietary regimes that have been claimed to help are the Feingold and 'K-P' diets. These exclude artificial additives, colourings and preservatives, as well as salicylates, a naturally occurring substance in certain foods. The scientific conclusion is that, just occasionally, the Feingold diet has been found to make a big difference in a child's behaviour, but usually there is no change, or else a small, short-lived change. One possibility for the failure of the Feingold diet could be that just removing additives is not enough. Children (particularly those with physical symptoms, like asthma and eczema) can react badly to all sorts of natural foods, not just those recommended for exclusion on the Feingold diet.

Trials at Great Ormond Street indicated with double-blind studies that carefully selected children react to certain foods with worsening behaviour. But would a wider range of children benefit? The only way to tell is through keeping a food diary, as I did, then excluding certain foods and judging which ones cause a reaction upon reintroduction. This can be a difficult process even with professional support.

Scientific views indicate that a few children are upset by certain foods, not because the food is toxic, but because the children have altered reactions. Caffeine is known to affect brain chemistry, and it tends to worsen irritable and restless behaviour in children. So it is worth cutting out tea, coffee and soft drinks containing caffeine if you suspect that they may affect your child's behaviour.

If parents decide to experiment with dietary treatments they need to use common sense and be wary of the pitfalls, such as the time and effort involved. Also, they should make sure that the diet does not add to the child's behaviour problems by causing him or her to feel deprived. Nor should they get on the treadmill of cutting out more and more foods, until the child ends up with an unbalanced diet. Beware of neglecting other treatments through being overly pre-occupied with the dietary treatment.

Dietary supplements

Some children, particularly those with autistic spectrum disorders, have very restricted diets and bizarre eating patterns. Many medical professionals claim that surveys indicate that, in most cases, their dietary intake and levels of minerals are adequate. Those illnesses that are caused by deficiencies are medically recognised. Iron is considered the most important, and deficiencies can cause learning and behaviour problems as well as anaemia.

Similar arguments apply to the use of vitamin supplements. If a child is particularly faddy, then supplements can be useful (with medical advice). Some parents claim to have seen behavioural improvements when they have flooded their child with nutrients or given vitamin therapy, or both. However, some vitamins, such as vitamins A and D, can be poisonous when taken in excess. The health food industry promotes vitamin and mineral supplements with the suggestion that they increase children's mental development. There is no scientific evidence yet to suggest that they help specific problems in children with learning disabilities and challenging behaviour.

Taking vitamins in large doses can act like drug therapy in altering brain chemistry. High doses of vitamin B6, often taken with magnesium, result in widespread chemical effects on the body. The treatment is not recommended for all autistic children because scientists are unsure about the balance between benefit and risk. Adverse effects appear to be rarer than those of other drug treatments. But, as a treatment, it is still in its experimental stages.

Physical interventions

David Allen, Consultant Clinical Psychologist at Cardiff Community Healthcare NHS Trust & Welsh Centre for Learning Disabilities, has written an information sheet about physical interventions for challenging behaviour. Some of what follows is based on what he wrote.

Because challenging behaviour tends to be a long-term problem, even with the best intervention plans in place, there are likely to be times when behaviour is out of control and when carers will be required to intervene to prevent damage to the person concerned or to themselves. In the absence of well-thought-out plans to manage out of control behaviours, the risks of injury for both parties are increased.

Reactive strategies provide carers with clear plans for how to respond to challenging behaviours. As their name suggests, they are 'reactive' in the sense that they are brought into play once challenging behaviours become apparent. Their use will not result in any future change in the pattern of a person's behaviour; their goal is simply to help carers achieve rapid, safe and effective control of out of control behaviours.

Because of these limitations, reactive strategies must never be used on their own, but as part of proactive, preventative plans for changing behaviour such as those I have mentioned earlier.

Despite the frequently held view that challenging behaviours occur 'out of the blue', most people show signs that they are becoming agitated or distressed before they lose control. Learning to recognise these early signs is the basis for early intervention, and the earlier carers intervene, the more probable it is that serious behavioural outbursts can be avoided.

Physical interventions should never be used until early signs of behavioural agitation have been responded to and proved ineffective. The term 'physical interventions' refers to 'any method of responding to challenging behaviour which involves some degree of direct physical force to limit or restrict movement or mobility' (Harris *et al.* 1996). Three broad categories of physical intervention may be identified:

- direct physical contact between a carer and a person with challenging behaviour (e.g. self-protective 'breakaway' techniques for escaping from grabs and chokes or minimal restraint to briefly immobilise the person)

- the use of barriers, such as locked doors, to limit freedom of movement

- the use of materials or equipment to restrict or prevent movement (e.g. the use of arm splints to reduce self-injury).

The use of physical intervention is an emotive topic which generates numerous ethical and practical concerns. Many care agencies shy away from considering this issue – despite the fact that physical interventions will almost certainly be used on an informal basis within any service supporting children or adults with severely challenging behaviour. Operating in a vacuum can be extremely dangerous, and agencies run the risk of failing to meet health and safety requirements if they do not train their staff adequately in this area. Last year, the Department of Health funded a project by the

British Institute of Learning Disabilities (BILD) and the National Autistic Society which sought to produce guidelines for agencies seeking to develop clear policies in this area. These are now available from BILD.

Some key principles from the document are that physical interventions

- should only be used in the best interests of the person with learning disabilities
- should only be used in conjunction with other strategies to help people learn to behave in non-challenging ways
- should be individualised and subject to regular review
- should employ minimal force and not cause pain.

Please note that there are another 28 principles in the document – and they are all equally important!

The law surrounding the use of physical interventions is also extremely complex. Fortunately, Professor Christina Lyon of the University of Liverpool has produced a detailed analysis of this area in work undertaken for the Mental Health Foundation (Lyon 1994). Although Professor Lyon's material is concerned with children, several of the general legal principles which she discusses also apply to adults.

The most prevalent form of training within the UK is 'control and restraint' (sometimes called 'care and responsibility'). This training was originally devised within the prison service, and was subsequently passed down into the special psychiatric hospitals, and from there into general psychiatric services and services for persons with learning disabilities. It is dependent on inflicting pain on the person presenting behavioural challenges for its effectiveness via a series of 'distraction' techniques and 'locks'. As the challenges presented by persons with learning disabilities are, not surprisingly, very different from those seen in prison populations, the ethics and legality of using this approach with the former group has been challenged (Allen *et al.* 1997). Although this training is often presented as being approved by the Home Office, it is not.

There are at least three forms of training within the UK at present which do not use pain-compliance methods and which clearly present reactive strategies in the context of proactive, positive approaches to challenging behaviour. These are:

- *Strategies for Crisis Intervention & Prevention (SCIP)*; contact: The Loddon School, Sherfield-on-Loddon, Nr Basingstoke, Hook, Hants RG27 0JD. Tel: 01256 882394.

- *Studio 111*; contact: Studio 111 Training Systems, 32 Gay Street, Bath BA1 2NT. Tel: 01752 254145.

- *Preventing & Responding to Aggressive Behaviour*; contact: Intensive Support Service, Welsh Centre for Learning Disabilities, Meridian Court, North Road, Cardiff CF4 3BL. Tel: 029-2061 5178.

A major weakness at present is that most training initiatives are directed to care agencies, with considerably less investment being made with parents.

It should be noted that the most prevalent form of intervention within services is probably chemical, not physical. Many persons with learning disabilities and challenging behaviour will be subject to high rates of medication, the primary role of which is to act as a behavioural suppressant rather than a treatment in the conventional sense. It is interesting to note that the use of chemical restraint has generally attracted less attention than physical restraint.

CHAPTER 22

How to Help Your Challenging Child

Practical help

Some of these ideas are taken from a leaflet (no longer available) produced by The Family Fund Trust. Others are taken from *Gentle Giant*, a book by the mother of an autistic child (Robinson 1999).

- To soothe a child in distress, music is helpful. The child may have his or her own cassette player, or a Walkman. Try the National Music and Disability Information Service (contact details on p.180).

- Consider making your child's room a calming environment by minimising clutter and irrelevant stimuli, and using soothing colours, sounds and smells.

- If your child wets and soils try the local health service continence adviser or the Enuresis Resource and Information Centre (ERIC) (contact details on p.178). Disposable nappies, plastic sheets, etc. may be available from the local Medical Supplies Department at your local health centre.

- To minimise damage to carpets and flooring try squirting from a soda siphon or washing with a solution of bicarbonate of soda. A product called 'Well Done' contains enzymes that digest and convert the waste, thus reducing the odour and leaving a more pleasant smell. The suppliers are: Certified Laboratories, PO Box 70, Oldbury, West Midlands B69 4AD. Cushionfloor covering or urine-proof heavy duty carpeting should be available from your local carpet shop.

- For head-banging, a safety helmet can be provided by the NHS.

- If the child is unaware of danger, lockable doors with security codes are a good way of restricting access to places like the kitchen. Wrought iron doors between the kitchen and living area enables you to see the child without him or her interfering with kitchen activities. Ask social services for help with this under the Chronically Sick and Disabled Persons Act. Cooker guards are available from British Gas, electricity companies and Mothercare.

- If the child fiddles with electrical plugs and switches, simply buy protective covers. Protective covers are available for electric sockets from your local electricity company, Mothercare or the charity SCOPE (contact details on p.181).

- If the child is 'into everything' remove sharp or dangerous objects and fit cupboard locks. Consider replacing furniture with sharp edges or fitting protective padding on the sharp edges, especially if your child self-injures.

- If the child hits people or things, consider making a punch bag and fasten to the door frame with a hook, as for a baby bouncer.

- For advice about equipment, contact your local social services department or the Disabled Living Foundation (contact details on p.178).

- Smearing excrement can be made more difficult for the child by dressing him or her in an all-in-one suit, either homemade or created from 'pull-on' type pyjamas sewn firmly together at the waist. An opening is made and reinforced down the back, just wide enough to squeeze the child through. The hole is then secured with buttons and tight loops or hooks and eyes. Showering with cold water can sometimes be effective!

- To protect windows and glass, Mothercare sells safety film.

- If your child has severe assaultive behaviours consider suitable clothes, e.g. wearing long sleeves can lessen the impact of a bite

on the forearm. It is not worth wearing your best clothes.
Clothing can get ripped and soiled. Jewellery can be grabbed
and pulled, and can cause injuries during a struggle.

Communication and challenging behaviour

The following ideas came from The Challenging Behaviour Foundation and Jill Bradshaw at the Tizard Centre, University of Kent.

Many people use the context and situation, rather than the actual
words used, to make sense of what is expected of them. If understanding skills are overestimated this may lead to confusions; for
example, if someone does not know what they are being asked to do
or if they receive the 'wrong message'.

Abstract and time concepts are particularly difficult to understand
and may lead to people not receiving the intended message. For
example:

> *Teacher's message – 'Sam, you're **not** going in the car.'*

> *Message understood by Sam – 'I'm going in the car.'*

Sam does not understand 'not' so thinks that he is going by car and
becomes distressed when he realises he will have to walk. The
message would have been clearer to Sam if the teacher had told him
what he *was* going to do: *'Sam, you're going for a walk.'*

People may also have difficulties because they are given too much
language to process and are only understanding key words. Many
people need to have information given to them in a simple structure.
For example:

> *Mother's message – 'Hannah, you can have a drink after you've tidied
> your room.'*

> *Message understood by Hannah – 'I'm having a drink and then tidying
> my room.'*

In English, what we say first is usually what we want the person to do
first. Hannah becomes upset when she is expected to tidy her room
and has not yet had her drink.

Another difficulty people may have is in interpreting language literally. We use many phrases whose intended meaning is not reflected in the actual words used. For example, if someone has done something that we find irritating we might say 'Oh, that's great!' when we actually mean the opposite. Understanding the intended meaning of such communication requires attention to tone of voice, facial expression and body language. These may not be understood by the child.

Many factors may contribute to the difficulties people with learning disabilities have in getting other people to understand them. The child may have difficulties in articulating speech or forming clear signs. They may lack the words necessary to convey the message they want to convey or they may use the right words but in the wrong order or without the appropriate supporting body language.

Such problems may be particularly crucial with certain sorts of messages. For example, indicating that an adult's request has not been understood, expressing a preference, letting someone know how you feel. If such important messages cannot be communicated, frustration is very likely and challenging behaviour may result. For example:

> John is asked to go shopping. He is unable to tell people that he is not in the mood to do this as he has had a busy morning. He would probably be happy to go after he has had a rest. He is unable to communicate these things and becomes upset and starts to scream when he is given his coat.

It is essential to have a good understanding of the ways in which a particular person communicates and of the ways in which information needs to be presented to them to facilitate their understanding. Challenging behaviour may be more likely to occur in situations where people either do not understand what is being expected or are unable to use communication to control their environment.

Other people need to make sure that they are communicating in a way that the person understands. This may include using simple, short sentences and trying to avoid saying something which could be misunderstood. Objects, pictures and symbols are particularly useful as ways of reminding people what will be happening throughout the day (being able to anticipate events is often important) and of supplementing spoken language. Signed communication is a useful supplement to spoken language too.

It is also important to respond consistently to what the person is trying to communicate (particularly when their means of communication is unclear). It may be possible to teach the individual an easier way of communicating; for example, by using visual communication. Additional vocabulary may need to be introduced, such as teaching the person how to ask for a rest.

Strategies to help a person communicate need to include all aspects of the individual's life and must include those people who regularly communicate to the person. This should include thinking about the communication issues overall and not just around situations where the challenging behaviour may occur.

I have recently heard about a computer program called Earobics that is mostly geared towards teaching children auditory discrimination. It can be used at home and at school. Because of the way it works, children stop and pay attention instead of impulsively choosing an answer. It is available from catalogues produced by the Edutainment Company (see their website on **www.edutain.co.com**). Another computer program that has been used for autistic children is Fast For Word. It is an intense way of improving speech levels and is used with a specialist teacher.

Experts you may come into contact with

The following are taken from two booklets published by Contact a Family (contact details on p.186): *Challenging Children – A Personal View* by Sheila Ramdular, and *Living Without a Diagnosis*.

audiologist – Works with children who have hearing difficulties and can advise on aids to improve hearing.

care manager – Assesses, organises and reviews the total care required for an individual. Can work for the local social services or the health authority.

children's community nurses – Not available in all areas. Responsible for carrying out certain nursing procedures and treatments at home. Can also advise families on caring for their child at home.

clinical medical officer (CMO) – Doctor who is present at child health clinics and who carries out school medical checks. In areas where there is not a community paediatrician (q.v.) available the CMO will co-ordinate services, and can initiate the statementing process, i.e. the process of obtaining a statement of Special Educational Needs (by which statutory provision is made for individual learning programmes at school).

clinical psychologist – Works with the child and family to help with any behavioural and developmental problems.

community paediatrician – Co-ordinates community health services and makes relevant referrals to other agencies. May be involved with the statementing process.

consultant – The most senior member heading a team of doctors. In overall charge of a child's care.

dietician/nutritionist – Will offer advice and help on special diets and feeding.

educational psychologist – Works with parents and teachers in assessing the psychological and educational needs of children with learning difficulties.

family therapist – Works with some or all of the family members, using the strength and commitment of the family to understand and deal more effectively with problems which any family member may be having. They are likely to want to see the family all together at least some of the time.

learning disabled assistants – These people are trained, but not qualified, teachers. They work in classrooms and playgrounds with children who need extra help in school.

MDT (multidisciplinary team) – A group of people usually working at or from the same base, who use their different professional skills and training to help the people they work with. A multi-disciplinary team might, for example, include a social worker, a nurse and a psychologist.

occupational therapist – Will help and advise on special aids and equipment, which will help in all areas of mobility and daily living.

orthoptist – Works with children who have squints, vision problems and abnormal eye movements.

paediatrician – Doctor who specialises in the care and treatment of children whilst in hospital, out-patients department or community setting.

physiotherapist – Uses exercise and movement to help the child gain as much independence as possible.

psychiatrist – A medical doctor who, after qualifying, has chosen to specialise in mental health and mental illness. It may be a psychiatrist who decides whether your child needs medication and who may prescribe it first.

social worker – Provides help and advice as well as emotional support with social and financial problems. Will also help to obtain local services such as respite care.

speech and language therapist – Works with children who are experiencing speech or language problems to enable them to communicate.

Useful addresses and telephone numbers

The following have mostly been obtained from Contact a Family's *Caring for Your Child: A Guide for Parents Who Care for a Child With a Disability or Special Needs* and *Challenging Children – A Personal View*, also published by Contact a Family.

Education

ACE (Advisory Centre for Education), 1b Aberdeen Studios, 22 Highbury Grove, London N5 2EA. Tel: 020-7354 8321. *Offers information and advice on all aspects of state education.*

Calibre Cassette Library, Aylesbury, Bucks HP22 5XQ. Tel: 01296-432339 *Free guidance and advice on all aspects of state education for people unable to read in the normal way.*

Independent Panel for Special Education Advice (IPSEA), 4 Ancient House Mews, Woodbridge, Suffolk IP12 1DU. Advice line: 01394-382814. *Independent advice for parents who are uncertain about, or disagree with, the LEA's interpretation of their child's special educational needs.*

Independent Special Education Advice – Scotland (ISEA), 164 High Street, Dalkeith EH22 1AY. Tel: 0131-454 0082. *Offers an advice line for people enquiring about special educational needs in Scotland.*

National Association of Toy & Leisure Libraries, 68 Churchway, London NW1 1LT. Tel: 020-7387 9592; Fax: 020-7383 2714. *Toy libraries lend good quality, carefully chosen toys to families with young children, including those with special needs. Also offer a befriending supportive service to parents and carers. Leisure libraries extend this concept to adults with special needs.*

National Portage Association, 127 Monks Dale, Yeovil BA21 3JE. Tel: 01935-471641. *Provides home learning schemes.*

Network 81, 1–7 Woodfield Terrace, Stansted, Essex CM24 8AJ. Helpline: 01279-647415 (10am – 2pm). *Information, guidance, help and advice on the Education Act and other procedures concerned with special educational provision.*

Pre-School Learning Alliance, 69 Kings Cross Road, London WC1X 9LL. Tel: 020-7833 0991; Fax: 020-7837 4942. *Contact their Special Needs Officer for information about playgroups for under-fives.*

TFH Special Needs, 76 Barracks Road, Sandy Lane Industrial Estate, Stourport-on-Severn, Worcs DY13 9QB. Tel: 01299-827820. *TFH (Toys for the Handicapped) produce mail order fun products and multisensory equipment for special needs children.*

Holidays

Camping for the Disabled, 20 Burton Close, Dawley, Telford, Shropshire TF4 2BX. Tel: 01743-761889; fax: 01743-761149. *Information and advice on camping and campsites in the UK and Europe.*

Family Holiday Association, 16 Mortimer Street, London W1N 7RD. Tel: 020-7436 3304. *Grants for families for one week's holiday of their choice. Applications received only from a health visitor, social worker or caring agency.*

Holiday Care Service, 2nd Floor, Imperial Building, Victoria Road, Horley, Surrey RH6 7PZ. Tel: 01293-774535; fax: 01293-784647; minicom: 01293-776943. *Information about all types of holidays for people with special needs.*

Make a Wish Foundation UK, Suite B, Rossmore House, 26–42 Park Street, Camberley, Surrey GU15 3PL. Tel: 01276-24127; fax: 01276-683727. *Can help fund or organise a special treat for children aged 3–18 with life threatening conditions.*

MENCAP Holiday Services, 119 Drake Street, Rochdale OL16 1PZ. Tel: 01706-54111. *Publishes an annual guide to holiday accommodation where people with learning disabilities are welcomed.*

National Holiday Fund for Sick and Disabled Children, Suite 1, Princess House, 1–2 Princess Parade, New Road, Dagenham, Essex RM10 9LS. Tel: 020-8595 9624. *Holidays for chronically or terminally ill children and temporarily or permanently physically disabled children, aged between eight and eighteen years.*

Starlight Foundation, 11–15 Emerald Street, London WC1N 3QL. Tel: 020-7430 1642; fax: 020-7430 1482. *Can help fund or organise a special treat for children with disabilities or special needs.*

Equipment and adaptations

Care and Repair, Castle House, Kirtley Drive, Nottingham NG7 1LD. Tel: 0115-979 9091. *Advice on adapting your home.*

Continence Foundation, 2 Doughty Street, London WC1N 2PH. Helpline: 020-7831 9831. *Information and advice on any aspect of incontinence.*

Disabled Living Centres Council, 1st Floor, Winchester House, 11 Cranmer Road, London SW9 6EJ. Tel: 020-7820 0567; fax: 020-7735 0278. *Centres across the country where you can see and try out aids and equipment.*

Disabled Living Foundation, 380–384 Harrow Road, London W9 2HU. Helpline: 0870-603 9177 *Information about aids and equipment.*

Enuresis Resource and Information Centre, 34 Old School House, Britannia Road, Kingswood, Bristol BS15 8DB. Helpline: 0117-960 3060; fax: 0117-960 0401; e-mail: enuresis@compuserve.com. *Advice on bladder incontinence. Published a guide for parents and carers of special needs children with bowel and bladder problems in 1999. Cost £3.50 inc. p&p.*

Royal Association for Disability and Rehabilitation (RADAR), 12 City Forum, 250 City Road, London EC1V 8AF. Tel: 020-7250 3222; fax: 020-7250 0212. *Advice on wheelchairs and other aids and equipment.*

Caring

Crossroads Care, 10 Regent Place, Rugby, Warwickshire CV21
2PN. Tel: 01788-573 653. And in Scotland: Crossroads
Scotland, 24 George Square, Glasgow G2 1EG. Tel: 0141-226
3793. *Care attendant schemes.*

National Association of Councils for Voluntary Services, 3rd Floor,
Arundel Court, 177 Arundel Street, Sheffield S1 2NU. Tel:
0114-278 6636. *Information about local Councils for Voluntary
Service, which can put volunteers in touch with people needing help.*

Financial

Disability Alliance Educational and Research Association, Universal
House, 88–94 Wentworth Street, London E1 7SA. Tel:
020-7247 8776; rights advice line: 020-7247 8763. *Information
and advice on benefits and help with filling in claim forms.*

Family Fund Trust, PO Box 50, York YO1 2ZX. Tel:
01904-621115. *Provides financial help for families looking after very
disabled children under sixteen. Publishes information leaflets on many
aspects of caring, including advice for disabled young people on
opportunities after the age of sixteeen.*

Legal advice

Children's Legal Centre, University of Essex, Wivenhoe Park,
Colchester CO4 3SQ. Tel: 01206-873820. *Provides advice on a
range of legal issues.*

Disability Law Service, Part 2nd Floor North, High Holborn House,
52–54 High Holborn, London WC1V 6RL. Tel: 020-7831
8031. *Legal advice.*

Family Advice Group, 18 Ashwin Street, London E8 3DL. Tel:
020-7923 2628. *Provides advice to parents in contact with social service
departments, especially on child protection issues.*

Other useful organisations

ADD/ADHD Family Support Group, 1a High Street, Dilton Marsh, Westbury. Tel: 01373-826045. *Offers support to parents and young people affected by ADD or ADHD whether or not they have been diagnosed.*

Association for All Speech Impaired Children (AFASIC), 347 Central Market, Smithfield, London EC1A 9NH. Helpline: 020-7236 3632. *AFASIC is the UK charity representing children and young adults with communication impairement, working for their inclusion in society and supporting their parents and carers.*

British Epilepsy Association, Anstey House, 40 Hanover Square, Leeds LS3 1BE. Tel: 0113 243 9393; helpline: 0808-800 5050. *Advice, information and support. Offers membership, campaigns and fundraises. Aims for a better future for people with epilepsy.*

CATCH! (Care and Action Trust for Children with Handicaps), Oystermouth House, Charter Court, Phoenix Way, Enterprise Park, Swansea SA7 9FS. Tel: 01792-790077. *CATCH! aims to provide services for families of a child with disabilities, and to bring about improvements to the present facilities offered by the social and welfare agencies. Also offers holidays to families in need of a break.*

Hyperactive Children's Support Group, 71 Whyke Lane, Chichester PO19 2LD. Tel: 01903-725182. *Offers support for hyperactive children and their families. It has a particular interest in diet and chemicals in food.*

MENCAP (Royal Society for Mentally Handicapped Children and Adults), 123 Golden Lane, London EC1Y 0RT. Tel: 020-7454 0454. *Information and support for carers of children with learning difficulties.*

National Autistic Society, 393 City Road, London EC1V 1NE. Tel: 020-7833 2299. *The Society provides support to people with autism and related developmental disorders, their families, carers and professional workers.*

National Music and Disability Information Service, Foxhole, Dartington, Totnes, Devon TQ9 6EB. Tel: 01449 736287. *Offers free advice and information to give people with disabilities chances to enjoy/be involved in/benefit from music.*

National Society for Epilepsy, Chesham Lane, Chalfont St Peter, Bucks SL9 0RJ. Tel: 01494-601300; helpline: 01494-601400. *Aims to advance research, treatment, care, support and understanding for people with epilepsy.*

SCOPE, 6–10 Market Street, London N7 9PW. Tel: 020-7619 7100; freefone helpline: 0800 626 216 (Monday to Friday 9am–9pm; weekends 2pm–6pm). *For people with cerebral palsy.*

SWAN (Syndromes Without a Name), 16 Achilles Close, Great Wyrley, Walsall WS6 6JW. Tel: 01922 701234. *National charity for undiagnosed children. Campaign for a greater awareness that these children exist, and therefore for greater support for children and their families.*

The Challenging Behaviour Foundation, 32 Twydall Lane, Gillingham ME8 6HX. Tel: 01634-302207. *A new organisation offering information for parents of children with severe learning difficulties and challenging behaviour.*

Young Minds, 102–108 Clerkenwell Road, London EC1M 5SA. Tel: 020-7336 8445; Parents Information Service: 0345-626 376. *A children's mental health charity offering telephone information to parents and producing a range of leaflets and resource sheets.*

General

Action for Sick Children, Argyle House, 29–31 Euston Road, London NW1 2SD. Tel: 020-7833 2041. *Supports families with sick children. Works to ensure effective planning of health services for children.*

Council for Disabled Children, National Children's Bureau, 8 Wakely Street, London EC1V 7QE. Tel: 020-7843 6061. *Provides information on children and disability issues, particularly Parent Partnership Schemes and Children's Disability Registers. Seeks to influence policy and practice.*

Family Welfare Association, 501–505 Kingsland Road, Dalston, London E8 4AU. Tel: 020-7254 6251. *Advice and information for people in need.*

Gingerbread, 16–17 Clerkenwell Close, London EC1R 0AA. Tel: 020-7336 8183. *Will put you in touch with local support and self-help groups for lone parents.*

I CAN (Invalid Children's Aid Nationwide), Barbican City Gate, 1–3 Dufferin Street, London EC1Y 8NA. Tel: 020-7374 4422. *Provides free help and advice to parents of disabled children.*

National Council for Voluntary Organisations (NCVO), Regents Wharf, 8 All Saints Street, London N1 9RL. Tel: 020-7713 6161. *Information about voluntary organisations.*

Parents at Work, 45 Beech Street, London EC2Y 8AD. Children with Disabilities Project helpline: 020-7588 0802 (Wednesday to Friday); information line: 020-7628 3578. *Information and advice about childcare provision to help working parents make the best choice of care for their child.*

Further Reading

Books and booklets

Clifton, J. and Glen, A. *Keeping Cheery Despite Setbacks: Handbook for Carers Working with People with Severe Learning Disabilities and Challenging Behaviours.* Barnardo's, 1992. ISBN: 0 9020 461 0 (£3.00). This handbook has been prepared to support carers who are entrusted with the care of people with severe learning difficulties and challenging behaviours and wish to provide that care in a creative yet structured and punishment free way.

Friel, J. *Young Adults with Special Needs: Assessment, Law and Practice – Caught in the Acts.* Jessica Kingsley Publishers, 1997 (4th edition). ISBN: 1 85302 231 4 (£14.95).
This enlarged and substantially revised edition updates the relevant legislation to take into account latest case law. The book has become established as the essential guide to educational rights of children with special needs.

Jackson, A. (ed) *Caring for Your Child.* Contact a Family, 1998. ISBN: 1 87374 710 1 (free).
A booklet describing assessment procedures, professionals parents come into contact with and useful voluntary organisations.

Jones, R. and Eayrs, C. (eds) *Challenging Behaviour and Intellectual Disability: A Psychological Perspective.* BILD, 1993 (Hardback), 1997 (Paperback). ISBN: (Hardback) 1 87379 120 8 (£49.95), (Paperback) 1 87379 163 1 (£14.95).
A collection of review articles by research workers with national and international reputations on the development of services to support people with learning disabilities and challenging behaviour.

Lyon, C. *Legal Issues Arising from the Care and Control of Children with Learning Disabilities Who Also Present Severe Challenging Behaviour: A Guide for Parents and Carers*. The Mental Health Foundation, 1994. ISBN: 0 90194 415 7 (£4.50).
A booklet for parents and carers which outlines the complicated legal issues surrounding the issue of restraint, which is sometimes used in services providing care for children with learning disabilities and/or challenging behaviour.

Menday, W., Partridge, L. and Shelley, P. *Living Without a Diagnosis*. Contact a Family, 1997. ISBN: 1 87471 524 6 (free with sae).
A factsheet aimed at parents who are caring for a child who does not currently have a diagnosis.

Mental Health Foundation. *Challenging Behaviour: What We Know*. 1995. ISBN: 0 90194 428 9 (£7.00).
The Mental Health Foundation believes that many people with learning disabilities and challenging behaviour are unnecessarily excluded from services. This publication aims to show how some services work, how they can improve and what effects they can have on people with learning disabilities and challenging behaviour and their parents and carers.

Mental Health Foundation. *Don't Forget Us: Report on Services for Children with Learning Disabilities and Severe Challenging Behaviour*. 1997. ISBN: 0 90194 442 4 (£12.00).
This report has been produced in response to the Mental Health Foundation's growing concern about the situation of children with learning disabilities and severe challenging behaviour. The Foundation has become increasingly aware of significant shortcomings in services to these children and their families.

National Autistic Society. *Your Child – Practical Help on How to Cope with Your Child's Challenging Behaviour*.
A leaflet containing an excerpt from the book *Autism: How to Help Your Young Child*.

Presland, J. *Overcoming Difficult Behaviour*. BILD, 1989. ISBN: 0
90605 467 2 (£15.95).
A comprehensive guide and sourcebook for helping people with
severe learning disabilities who present challenging behaviours. In
four sections: 'Introduction to behavioural approaches'; 'A guide to
action'; 'Specific problems'; and 'Making it possible'.

Qureshi, H. 'Impact on families: Young adults with learning
disability who show challenging behaviour.' In C. Kiernan (ed)
*Research to Practice: Implications of Research on the Challenging
Behaviour of People with Learning Disability*. BILD, 1993. ISBN: 1
87379 125 9 (£19.95).
Young adults with learning disabilities who show challenging
behaviour are a key group in relation to policies for community care.
The presence of behaviour problems has been shown to be an
important factor influencing levels of stress in family carers and
decisions to place people in residential care. Doubts have been
expressed about whether community-based services are able to cope
with young people in this group or offer sufficient support to parents
in circumstances where permanent admission to hospital is far less
likely to be available than in the past. The findings reported in this
paper are derived from a study of the parents of 59 young adults who
were identified by staff in services as showing challenging behaviour
during the course of a large scale epidemiological study described
elsewhere in the same volume.

Ramdular, S. *Challenging Children – A Personal View*. Contact a Family,
1998. ISBN: 1 87471 526 2 (£5.00 + £0.50 p&p).
A booklet written by a parent of a child with challenging behaviour
and ADHD.

Articles

Articles on challenging behaviour that have proved interesting
reading are:

'My life with Ursula: A sister's tale'; published in *Community Living*
in April 1996. It describes what it is like living with a sibling
who has challenging behaviour from the viewpoint of

Ursula's sister, Charlotte Clancy Smith, aged 13. She describes a typical week in her life and the strategies she has used to cope with the unpredictability of Ursula's behaviour.

'Changing behaviours' by Julie Colsey and Angela Hatton; published in the *Nursing Times* in September 1994 (volume 90, no. 39). The authors describe the approach their team took to helping a family with a child who had frequent tantrums.

'Facing the challenge' by Hazel Qureshi; published in the *Nursing Times* in November 1990 (volume 86, no. 45). It asks how parents can deal with violent outbursts from their mentally handicapped children once they are grown up. Do they feel supported by community mental handicap nurses?

Addresses for further reading material

Barnardo's, Yorkshire Division, 'Four Gables', Clarence Road, Horsforth, Leeds, West Yorkshire LS18 4LB. Tel: 0113-258 2115.

British Institute of Learning Disabilities (BILD), Wolverhampton Road, Kidderminster, Worcestershire, DY10 3PP. Tel: 01562 850251.

Contact a Family, 170 Tottenham Court Road, London W1P 0HA. Tel: 020-7383 3555.

Mental Health Foundation, 20–21 Cornwall Terrace, London, NW1 4QL. Tel: 020-7535 7400.

Jessica Kingsley Publishers, 116 Pentonville Road, London N1 9JB. Tel: 020-7833 2307.

References

Allen, D. (1997) 'Changing care staff approaches to the prevention and management of aggressive behaviour in a residential treatment unit for persons with mental retardation and challenging behaviour.' *Research in Developmental Disabilities 18*, 2, 101–112.

Corbett, J., Murphy, G. and Oliver, C. (1987) 'Self-injurious behaviour in people with mental handicap: A total population study.' *Journal of Mental Deficiency Research 31*, 147–162.

Crockenberg, S. (1981) 'Infant irritability, mother responsiveness, and social support influences on the security of infant–mother attachment.' *Child Development 52*, 857–865.

Dosen, A. and Gielen, J. (1993) 'Depression in person with mental retardation: Assessment and diagnosis.' In A. Dosen and A. Fletcher (eds) *Mental Health Aspects of Mental Retardation*. New York: Lexington Books.

Emerson, E., Barrett, S., Bell, C., Cummings, R., Toogood, A. and Mansell, J. (1987) *Developing Services for People with Severe Learning Difficulties & Challenging Behaviours*. Canterbury: University of Kent.

Graham, P., Rutter, M. and Yule, W. (1970) *A Neuropsychiatric Study in Childhood*. Spastics International Medical Publications. London: Heinemann.

Greene, L., Neal, B., Newey, D., Wraith, E. and Vellodi, A. (1992) 'Parents and professionals – Are we communicating?' In H. Marsh (ed) *A Conference Report*. London: Contact a Family.

Harris, J., Cornick, M., Jefferson, A. and Mills, R. (1996) 'Physical restraint procedures for managing challenging behaviours presented by mentally retarded adults and children.' *Research in Developmental Disabilities 16*, 2, 99–134.

Hemsley, R. and Taylor, E. (1990) 'Research section: Dietary treatment in autism and hyperactivity.' *Communication 24*, 2. London: National Autistic Society.

Hurley, A. and Sovner, R. (1983) 'Do the mentally retarded suffer from affective illness?' *Archives of General Psychiatry 40*, 61–67.

Lyon, C. (1994) *Legal Issues Arising from the Care of Children with Learning Disabilities Who Also Present Severe Challenging Behaviour.* London: Mental Health Foundation.

Marcheschi, M., Masi, G. and Pfanner, P. (1998) 'Depression in adolescents with mental retardation: A clinical study.' *British Journal of Developmental Disabilities 44*, 2, 87.

Menday, W., Partridge, L. and Shelley, P. (1997) *Living Without a Diagnosis.* London: Contact a Family.

Miller, K. and Reynolds, W. (1985) 'Depression and learned helplessness in mentally retarded and non-mentally retarded adolescents: An initial investigation.' *Applied Research in Mental Retardation 6*, 295–306.

Murray, L., Stanley, C., Hooper, R., King, F. and Fiori-Cowley, A. (1996) 'The role of infant factors in postnatal depression and mother–infant interactions.' *Developmental Medicine and Child Neurology 38*, 109–119.

Prisms (Parents & Researchers Interested in Smith–Magenis Syndrome) (1992) *What is Smith–Magenis Syndrome?* Leaflet.

Reiss, S. (1990) 'Prevalence of dual diagnosis in community-based day programs in the Chicago metropolitan area.' *American Journal on Mental Retardation 94*, 578–585.

Robinson, W. (1999) *Gentle Giant: The Inspiring Story of an Autistic Child.* Shaftesbury, Dorset: Element Books.

Shattock, P., Kennedy, A., Rowell, F. and Berney, T.P. (1990) 'Role of neuropeptides in autism and their relationships with classical neuro transmitters.' *Brain Dysfunction 3*, 328–345.

Wertheimer, A. (ed) (1997) *Do not Forget Us.* London: Mental Health Foundation.